Comforts of Home

The Best of Today's Creative Home Arts

CREATIVE
HOME
ARTS
—CLUB—

Creative Home Arts Library™

Introduction

Many Club Members save all their issues of *Today's Creative Home Arts* magazine. It's easy to tuck each copy into a bin or a binder for future reference, once you're done working from it. But it's not always easy to remember where you saw projects you liked and created and want to make again, or to find projects you saw in past issues and thought, "I want to make that someday."

With this book, we've made both processes easier for you. **Comforts of Home** collects more than 50 favorite projects from *Today's Creative Home Arts* magazine, and puts them in one convenient, easy-to-reference place. We have selected the projects Members liked the best! Organized into five chapters, **Comforts of Home** gives you craft, decorating and gift projects that will help you make your home even more unique and comfortably personal.

In the **Casual Style** chapter, you'll find a dozen simple ways to add a stamp of individuality to everyday items. The projects in the **Natural Beauty** chapter show you how to bring the outdoors inside, and how to create a sense of home in your outdoor spaces. **Mementos & Gifts** is full of projects you can make to shower yourself or your friends with thoughtful, meaningful presents. In the **Holiday Events** chapter, projects focus on special details that will make your holidays more memorable. For ideas that offer a final touch, turn to **Classic Decorating**, where the projects are the proverbial icing on the cake.

Throughout these pages, you will find beautiful photos of the finished projects, along with the clear step-by-step instructional photography that you expect and depend on.

Almost everything about crafting and decorating comes down to making your home a more comfortable, attractive and pleasing place to live. We want Members like you to experience success in all your projects, and to find great joy in the **Comforts of Home**.

CREATIVE
HOME
ARTS
—CLUB—

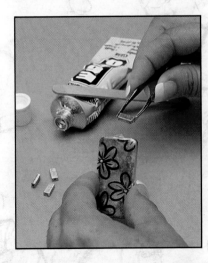

Casual *Style*

From the furniture and wall hangings you choose to the color of your bath towels, your home reflects your personal tastes. Here are a dozen projects that give you even more ideas for personalizing every room in your home.

Coordinate an old dresser with your room's décor. Transform an old table runner or dresser scarf into unique "new" curtains. Create unique pillows from old sweaters, or by adding an appliqued design. What you can do with a little paint or needle and thread will surprise you and motivate you to decorating success!

A Dressed-up *Dresser*

Turn a dull piece of furniture into a gorgeous decorative accent with these tricks.

Everyone can always use more shelves, drawers, and closets. Sometimes, however, the furniture we're forced to press into service can be more functional than fabulous. This old dresser was sturdy, spacious, a good size, and—ugly. It is made of a material called MDF, which is a pressed wood product commonly used in inexpensive furniture.

We wanted to keep the dresser but were tired of its humdrum appearance. We found a way to freshen up the look in a couple of hours for less than $30 in materials, using as our focal point FabriCraft, a new adhesive-backed fabric that is applied much like shelf paper.

You Will Need

- Old dresser
- Screwdriver
- 220-grit sandpaper
- Primer (we used Zinsser 1-2-3)
- Drill and drill bit (size depends on drawer hardware size)
- Duct tape
- Wood filler and spatula
- Semigloss paint
- Paintbrush and small roller
- Measuring tape or ruler
- Scissors or self-healing mat and rotary cutter
- FabriCraft adhesive fabric
- Wood molding (available at home improvement stores)
- Paint
- Miter box
- Hot-glue gun and glue

Getting Started

Remove hardware from drawers and set aside. Lightly sand and prime the entire dresser.

1 NOTE: FabriCraft adhesive-backed fabric comes in 18-inch widths. Because of the design of our dresser, we wanted our hardware to appear inside the fabric area we planned for the front of our dresser. Since our existing hardware fell outside this line, we removed it and redrilled holes to replace it where we wanted it. If this doesn't apply to your piece, skip to Step 3.

Measure and drill new holes for hardware placement on drawer fronts. TIP: The drawer pull is a great measurement tool to use for placing the new holes.

4 To create an opening for drawer hardware, clip fabric using small scissors. TIP: Use the closed tip of the scissors to flatten the fabric inside the holes.

2 Place duct tape behind the holes in the dresser that need to be filled. Fill the holes with wood filler. Allow wood filler to dry, then sand. (You may need to repeat this step, since the wood filler shrinks when it dries.) TIP: Touch up the filled area with primer before painting the dresser.

Paint the dresser and drawers with two coats of semigloss paint.

5 Cut wood molding to fit around the fabric edge of the drawer front. Cut corners at a 45-degree angle using a miter box. Hot-glue trim in place starting along the top edge, then the sides and bottom. TIP: Use the edge of the fabric as a gluing guide. It also helps to have a small square to ensure that the side trim pieces are kept straight.

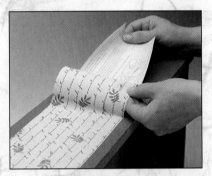

3 Measure the drawer front to determine the placement of the FabriCraft. Here we centered the FabriCraft on the drawer. We also left an inch of space along the top and bottom edge of the drawer to allow for placement of decorative trim.

Lightly mark the placement of the fabric on the drawer front using a sharp pencil and ruler. (The pencil marks will be covered later with wood trim. Cut pieces of the FabriCraft equal to these measurements for each drawer.)

Peel off about 4 inches of backing paper and line up fabric with marked measurements. Once this starter edge is positioned, gently peel back the remainder of the paper, smoothing the fabric as you go. (It can be repositioned if needed.) TIP: We found that rolling up the FabriCraft made it easier to position on the drawer front.

SPECIAL PROJECT TIPS

- FabriCraft comes in several complementary patterns that can be used alone or together. (We used one from the Nurturing Garden Collection.) Find FabriCraft at your craft store or visit www.deltacrafts.com for more information.

A Personal *Stamp*

Use rubber stamps to turn inexpensive dinnerware into gorgeous, coordinated serving pieces.

Finding a way to turn inexpensive materials into one-of-a-kind treasures can be a thrill.

In this project, you can turn plain glass plates (which can often be found very inexpensively at your local "everything-for-a-dollar" store) into unique decorative accents. Better yet, this project is so simple that you can make a dozen matching pieces, or create only one or two to highlight a special occasion.

These decorative plates make beautiful serving pieces, or you can use the same technique to make coasters, candle stands, and more. (These plates can be used for food, but they won't stand up to being immersed in water or put through the dishwasher. The plates must be hand washed, on the surface only, to protect the design on the back side.)

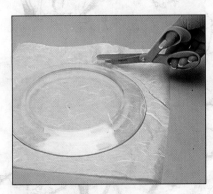

1 Cut a square of mulberry paper slightly larger than the size of your plate. Lay the mulberry paper flat on your work surface with the textured side down. This will make stamping easier. Lay your glass plate on the mulberry paper and use a scissors to trim the paper to size. Set the plate aside for now.

Place the circle of mulberry paper on a protected surface to prepare for stamping.

Special Project Tips

- Use this technique to make your own serving platters, dessert plates, coasters, or even glass candle bases. Any smooth surface will work! You can try different colors of mulberry paper and different ink colors (even metallic ink works well).

- You can use napkins or printed tissue paper for your patterned background instead of stamping.

2 Examine the stamps you will be using and mentally lay out your design. (TIP: If you are using larger images, plan to have some of them run partially off the mulberry paper. This will give you a more balanced, finished work. Smaller images can be stamped around the edge of the plate for a border or frame.)

Ink your stamp images well with permanent or crafters' ink. (Remember not to use standard ink pads, as the images may bleed when moistened.) Stamp your images across the surface of the mulberry paper, making sure to apply good pressure to your stamp.

(When stamping with a crafters' ink pad, use a heat tool or iron set to low, to heat-set the stamped images for 10 to 15 seconds. If you are using a heat tool, move the tip of the tool evenly over your stamped images, being careful not to burn the paper. If you are ironing the paper, try the iron on a small section first, so that you'll know how long to iron without scorching. A piece of paper toweling placed between the mulberry paper and your iron is helpful.)

3 Using a sponge-tipped brush, cover the back side of the plate with a thin, even coat of Mod Podge. Carefully lay the stamped mulberry paper over the Mod Podge, so that the stamped images can be seen through the glass plate. Gently press the paper onto the plate to remove any air bubbles and ease out any folds. Be careful not to tear the paper. (TIP: The fibers in the mulberry paper will help mask any folds that are difficult to remove.) Using a moistened paper towel, clean up any Mod Podge that has smeared on the front side of the plate. Once the adhesive dries, it is difficult to remove, so be sure to catch any drips now.

Allow plate to dry slightly before proceeding to the next step.

4 With your scissors, trim the mulberry paper as close to the edge of the plate as you can. Trim any thicker fibers with a scissors. Don't pull them, as this may tear the paper. Using the craft knife, carefully remove any excess fibers from the edge of your plate. Press the raw edge of the paper to the plate.

Next, brush the back of the mulberry paper with a coat of Mod Podge. The wet mulberry paper will tear easily, so be careful. Inspect edges from time to time to ensure that the cut edge of the mulberry paper stays glued to the plate. Allow the plate to dry for about 15 minutes before applying another coat of Mod Podge. Repeat two more times, allowing layers to dry between coats. Allow the plate to dry thoroughly and spray only the back of the plate with a clear acrylic sealer. Don't soak your finished plate in water, and don't put it in the dishwasher. Surface wash only.

Second Life

Turn a worn-out sweater into an adorable throw pillow, complete with decorative details.

There's a thrifty Yankee saying that holds, "Use it up, wear it out, make it do, or do without." That's a sentiment that fits perfectly with the idea behind these attractive throw pillows. You probably have a least a few favorite old sweaters that either no longer fit or have small worn spots that may once have made them destined for the rag bag.

With a little creativity, however, you can use the materials from these sweaters to make dozens of decorative throw pillows.

The possibilities for this easy little project are endless. You can incorporate details from your sweaters directly into your pillows, depending on how you cut your fabric. Consider leaving the buttons on the material, and you have a "fitted" throw pillow with little work. Or leave a pocket on the front for a little added dash.

This project can be accomplished in less than an hour, for under $20 in materials.

1 Cut a piece of lining fabric equal to the size of the pillow form you will be using. Using the lining as your pattern, cut the sweater and the fabric for the back of the pillow.

2 If your sweater has a button front such as ours, sew the button front closed. Pin the sweater to the lining, wrong sides together. Stitch together using ¼-inch seam allowance.

3 Pin the trim to the right side of the fabric being used for the back of the pillow, lining up the edge of the trim with the raw edge of the fabric. Sew in place using ¼-inch seam allowance. Pin the front to the back, right sides together. Sew in place using ½-inch seam allowance, leaving an opening to turn fabric right side out.

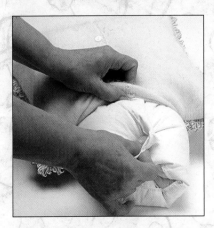

4 Insert the pillow form and hand stitch the opening closed.

You Will Need

- Old sweater
- Pillow form to fit the sweater you select
- ½-yard lining fabric
- ½-yard coordinating fabric for the back of the pillow
- 1½ to 2 yards trim
- Scissors
- Pins
- Measuring tape

SPECIAL PROJECT TIP

- Old sweaters make cozy pillows, and are a great way to save a worn favorite by remaking it into something new.

Girly Fun

Make any little girl feel like a star with this decorated wastebasket.

Want to make a favorite little someone feel like a star? Try this fun and funky decorated wastebasket, which uses stamps, craft painting, and a little glitter for great results.

1 Wash and dry trash can. Using primer designed for use on plastic, paint the entire can. (This will help ensure that the paint adheres well to the surface.) Let dry.

On a piece of aluminum foil, mix white acrylic paint with a small amount of fuchsia to make pink.

Using a sea sponge, dab paint all around trash can. Let dry to touch; then, using the sea sponge, dab white acrylic randomly over first coat. Let dry completely.

Girly Fun Dancing Pattern
Enlarge pattern 300% for the wastepaper basket and 275% for the child's quilt on next page.

2 Trace pattern of girl on tracing paper using a soft lead pencil. Flip over the pattern and trace lines again, pressing firmly. Flip over again with right side up and position on can. Use a small piece of tape to secure if needed. Retrace lines to transfer pattern.

4 Paint girl's dress and shoes with fuchsia. Let dry.

On reverse side of can, loosely freehand "I am a" in fuchsia with brush. Apply same color to large star stamp and stamp following the words.

Apply turquoise craft paint to a single small star from the grouping and stamp randomly around the trash can. Wash and dry stamp. Stamp three small stars in white on girl's dress.

Lightly pencil in features on girl's face and outline with black dimensional fabric paint. Dip a cotton swab in the pink mixture and dot cheeks. Loosely line around "I am a" and the large fuchsia stars.

3 Add tiny dab of orange to the pink mixture to create a flesh tone. Paint girl's face, arms, and legs.

On a clean piece of foil, pour a puddle of orange craft paint. Tap the flat end of the sponge into the paint and pounce onto the swirl stamp. Stamp swirl on each side of girl's head, applying paint for each stamping. Pounce orange on only the small stars of the star group stamp. Stamp on top of head between the swirls. Wash and dry stamps.

5 Make dots using diamond glitter fabric paint in stars above girl's face and place a gemstone in centers. Make a glitter line inside the swirls of the girl's hair and in center of blue stars and around fuchsia stars.

Glue trim around rim of trash can and hem of girl's dress.

Rise and Shine *Bedspread*

Use stamps and fabric dyes to make a fun bedspread for a youngster in your life.

To add variety to this fun painting and stamping project, we created these alternate turquoise squares on individual pieces of white fabric. (See Special Project Tip.)

For a less-involved project, make a single throw pillow by creating only one stamped square sewed to a plain backing.

Getting Started

Prewash fabric. Do not use fabric softener. Shake all bottles of paint well.

Photocopy pattern from page 15 to desired size. Trace over lines on reverse side of pattern with a pencil. Turn right-side-up and place pattern on card stock. Trace over lines again to transfer pattern to card stock.

Cut out pattern with a craft knife to create a stencil.

3 Pour orange fabric paint on palette and stamp two swirls on the sides of girl's face. Dab paint only on small stars of Star Group. Stamp between swirls for top of hair. Let dry. Draw in features and outline girl using black dimensional fabric paint. Let dry.

Place paper towels around square with girl. Spray lightly around girl with Hot Pink Cool Color Spray, spraying mainly around edges.

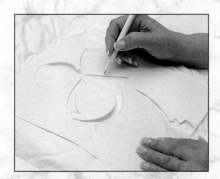

1 Trace inside stencil on fabric using a disappearing ink pen for fabric. (If you are using separate fabric squares for either a pillow or a quilt, you can complete all of the tracings at once. If you are applying this pattern to a pre-made bedspread, you'll want to transfer the pattern to every other square area, starting at the top of bedspread. On the next rows, place the pattern between top images alternating the placement of the girl. Trace. Repeat over entire bedspread.)

2 Tape around the edge of your fabric square to keep edges clean. (If you are working directly on a bedspread instead of using separate fabric squares, place paper towels around areas to be painted to prevent paint spatters on bedspread.)

Mix equal parts white and peach fabric paint on a palette to make a flesh tone. Brush in face, arms, and legs.

Pour enough rose-pink fabric paint on palette to paint dress and shoes. Repeat, painting all squares with girl.

4 Using pink dimensional fabric paint, make thin squiggle lines 1 inch from edge of square. Use clean paper and press on line, one side at a time, using clean sheet for each press. TIP: To save on paper towels, fold wet paint edge to inside of paper towel.

SPECIAL PROJECT TIP

- Pour turquoise fabric paint on palette. Lay out fabric squares on protected work surface. Dab paint sponge into paint and dab excess on palette. Dab paint on large star stamp. Stamp image a little off center on each square. Let dry. Outline the outside of Star stamp on fabric using Cool Color Block. Make swirls around star (refer to picture). Let dry several hours or until set—see manufacturer's instructions. Once dry, spray star-stamped squares with Caribbean Blue, let dry, and then wash. Turn edges under ½ inch and press. Secure turned edge with fusible hemming or sew in place. Add white buttons to corners for a decorative touch. Finish your spread by randomly stamping additional images throughout.

Instant *Updates*

Personalize any ready-made item with super-simple transfers that look like hand-painted art.

Some of the virtues of chain stores are consistent quality, clever products, and useful items that make any house more decorative. Unfortunately, one of the downsides to these same superstores is that the items we purchase there don't necessarily reflect our personal taste.

However, updating ready-made items is both easy and fun. For this simple project, we used a bookshelf we purchased inexpensively as the platform for a swarm of fall butterflies using rub-on transfers. We further accessorized by using the same rub-ons on several other items to create a small but unified corner in our home.

1 Remove the glass frames from the bookshelf. On alternate windows, measure and then cut decorative paper to fit the frame openings.

2 Cut out selected designs from the rub-on transfer and remove backing sheet. Position on project design-side up. Rub over design firmly with craft stick to transfer image. Lift sheet.

SPECIAL PROJECT TIP

- Rub-on transfers are inexpensive but loaded with fun. For instance, transfers offer specialized designs for different seasons, including pumpkins, ghosts, and colorful leaves for fall, or a variety of festive subjects that are perfect for Christmas and the holiday season. The Tulip transfers we used are also acid-free, photo-safe and non-yellowing, so they're also perfect for scrapbooks and other paper crafts.

SPECIAL PROJECT TIP

- Rub-on transfers are perfect for scrapbooking and other papercrafts, but they will also adhere to almost any clean dry surface. We used the remaining butterflies from our rub-on sheet to add a personal touch to a candle and to a few decorative glass bottles that we used to hold bath oil.

Vintage *Memories*

Transform a delicate old dresser scarf into a clever curtain designed to let in light.

Beautiful old linens abound in antique stores, at flea markets, and sometimes even tucked away inside drawers in a home. These old-world beauties often sport elegant handwork or lace and are a gorgeous reminder of a time when a woman's skill with a needle was viewed as an important gauge of her skill as a homemaker.

There's a way to take advantage of these beautiful linens by transforming them into less formal, "everyday" items that can be displayed with pride.

In this case, we pulled a dainty dresser scarf with beautifully finished ends out of storage and put it into day-to-day use as a café curtain in a bathroom. (We also found a way to make use of an old pair of sheer curtains in this project to minimize the sewing involved, making this an extra-quick redo.)

Getting Started

Measure your window to determine the finished length of your café curtain. Our finished length was 30 inches.

We could have simply cut our dresser scarf to size for this window and completed our sewing, but since the curtain was meant for a second floor and didn't need to provide privacy, we maximized the amount of light that could come through by adding a 7-inch sheer top to the piece. (This is a great way to get more light in a space.) We used a premade sheer and made use of the hemmed edges and the existing rod pocket.

You Will Need

- Dresser scarf or old table runner
- Sheer drapery panel
- Measuring tape
- Scissors
- Pins
- Iron
- Seam ripper
- Fusible hem

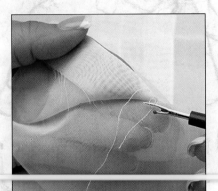

1 Fold sheer drapery panels in half along the width, lining up the sides and top. Pin in place. Measure down from the top edge of the sheer panel to your desired length, adding ½ inch for seam allowance. Mark with fabric marker and cut. Measure width of dresser scarf and add 2 inches. Cut sheer fabric equal to this measurement. **TIP:** Remember to leave one side with a finished hem. Cut dresser scarf to desired finished length plus ½ inch for seam allowances.

2 Using a seam ripper, remove about 4 inches of stitching along the casing of your sheer, starting on the unfinished edge. Make a double 1-inch hem along the side of the sheer. Pin and sew in place, keeping stitches as close to the folded inside edge as possible. To finish, sew casing for rod pocket following existing sewing lines.

3 With right sides together, pin sheer top to the dresser scarf, aligning raw edges. **TIP:** Insert several pins to keep fabric from shifting. Sew in place using ½-inch seam allowance. Press seam down toward bottom edge.

4 Insert fusible hem between the sheer and the linen. Press following manufacturer's instructions. (This will keep the raw edges from fraying.)

A Chair
with a *Flair*

Update an old chair with a new coat of paint and decorative raised stencil designs.

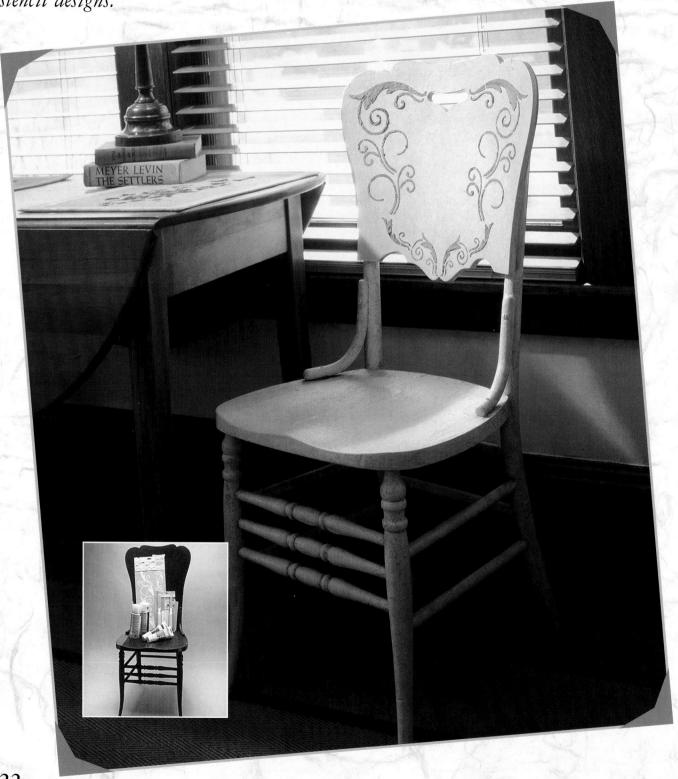

Vintage chairs have unique charm. You can find these old beauties at numerous yard, estate, and tag sales, often for only a few dollars. Whether they are one-of-a-kind accent pieces or lonely survivors of a matched set, single chairs are always useful—and surprisingly decorative.

We found this old chair at a local yard sale and decided to refashion it into an accent piece with a new coat of paint and decorative, raised designs. We created our stencil using a product called Texture Magic by Delta Technical Coatings. This lightweight, creamy material can be spread over a

stencil like cake frosting. When dry, it leaves a raised design on any flat surface. (You can even mix several colors of the product together, as we did, to create a swirled mix of colors on your stencil in only one step.)

Getting Started

Be certain that the chair you've selected is sturdy. Refasten peeling veneer by squirting wood glue underneath the loosened section and then clamping until dry. Reglue any loose pegs and make any other adjustments necessary to ensure that the piece is sound.

Sand, prime, and paint the chair with two coats of paint in a shade of your choice.

You Will Need

- Wood chair
- 220-grit sandpaper
- Primer (we used Zinsser 1-2-3)
- Semigloss paint (we used a shade of off white)
- Paintbrush
- Stencil (ours was a pattern called Wrought Iron Scroll)
- Stencil spray adhesive
- Scissors
- Painter's tape
- Texture Magic
- Small spatulas
- Polyurethane spray

Optional:
- Glazing medium and burnt umber tint
- Feather duster

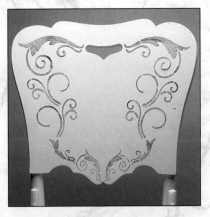

3 Continue to work with the different elements of the stencil until you have achieved your finished look. This piece was created using and reusing the elements from one stencil.

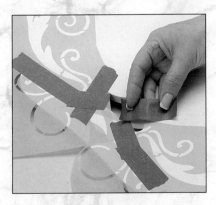

1 Plan the stencil design for the back of your chair. If the chair will be used for extra seating, and not just as a decorative item, keep in mind that the design should be placed to the outside edge of the chair back.

TIP: Cutting a stencil into pieces makes it easier to work with when you're creating mirror-image designs. You may also have to work on only one section of the chair at a time if you plan to reuse the same stencil in different locations.

Spray the back side of the stencil with adhesive and place on the chair. Tape off any areas that you do not want to use in your design.

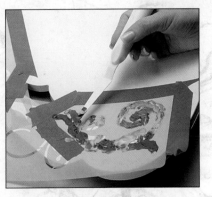

2 Following manufacturer's instructions, squeeze Texture Magic onto stencil. (We used two complementary colors to create the design for our project. Using two colors adds depth and additional dimension to the finished piece.) TIP: Darker hues go a long way—use them sparingly at first since you can always add more.

Using a spatula or similar tool, gently smear the two colors together, creating a thin textured layer over the openings on the stencil. (The process is much like frosting a cake.)

Remove stencil and let design dry. Clean the stencil and tools immediately after use.

4 We decided to apply an antiquing glaze to our chair to give it an aged appearance.

Mix about ½ cup of glaze with two teaspoons of burnt umber tint. Working in small sections, brush on the glazing mixture with a paintbrush. You can dab an old feather duster directly onto the brushed-on glaze to create additional texture and remove any excess. (You can also use a soft cloth to remove the glaze by softly dabbing the cloth over the wet surface.)

Once the chair has dried completely, spray on a coat of glossy polyurethane to protect the glaze and seal the chair.

5 minutes and Fabulous

Want to throw a perfect party? Try these clever ideas for unusual napkin rings.

There's something about using real cloth napkins that makes any meal feel like an event. You can make a dinner or a party feel even more special with one of the little tricks shown here that turn easy-to-find items into clever napkin rings. Your guests will think you're a creative genius—and you won't have spent a bundle to make an impression!

Casual Comfort

Cloth napkins don't have to mean a formal, sit-down dinner for 12. In fact, this napkin "ring" is the epitome of casual—a chunky coffee mug with a large handle. Simply fold the napkin in an accordion pleat, double it over, and stick the fold through the handle of your favorite cup. Fun and festive, and the eye appeal it provides is huge.

Personal Perfection

This idea does triple duty—it serves as a place card, letting your guests know where you'd like them to sit; it doubles as a napkin ring; and it gives each guest a little "present from the hostess" as they leave.

To make these, you'll need a bag of mixed letter beads from your local craft store and some fabric cord used to make jewelry. (You can find economy-sized bags of letter beads for only a couple of dollars.) Simply spell out the names of your guests, string the beads on the cord, and loop enough around each napkin to let your guests turn these into a cute necklace or bracelet later.

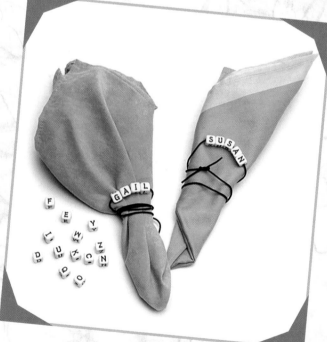

Rustic Rodeo

Who said napkins must be white damask or needy linen? Pocket kerchiefs make fabulous large napkins that are perfect for a backyard barbecue. Wrap them with a few twists of rawhide cord and toss them in a basket for a splash of color and a hint of the fun to come.

Wedding Rings

If a wedding is in your future—whether it's yours or a loved one's—make a stop at your local wedding or craft store and pick up a bag of thin, lightweight wedding rings. (These come in huge bags for a couple of dollars.) Pick up a spool or two of ribbon in the bride's colors, as well. Then simply tie a bow around a napkin and string two of the rings together on top. The effect is wonderfully simple but very elegant.

Antique Class

Why not playfully celebrate the reason you've gathered with a food-centered napkin holder? Old-fashioned, thin-handled utensils work best for this idea. (Your local antique store or flea market will have dozens of mismatched spoons, forks, and knives that you can mix-and-match for very little cash.)

Gently bend the handle of the utensil backward until it nearly touches its own handle and slip it over the end of your napkin.

A Garden Party

Simple, simple, simple, but cute, cute, cute.

It seems that spare silk flowers have a way of accumulating in any home. Then there are the bargain bins at the local craft store screaming "70 percent off" on elegant stems that make us itch to gather an armload.

Here's a very quick way to add a little punch to any party. Simply twist the stem of one of those silk lovelies into a rough circle (the bendable wire inside makes this easy) and slip it around your favorite napkin.

Braided *Past*

Old-fashioned crafts offer an up-to-date look at a price that's just right.

In the 1930s and 40s, braided rugs were more of a thrifty necessity than a hobby. That era was also when my grandmother was making room-sized braided rugs for her family of 12.

My mother and her sisters made use of scraps of old fabric and worn-out clothes by cutting the fabric into strips, folding them, and then stitching those bits and pieces together on a treadle sewing machine. When grandmother finally had enough strips, she would start braiding.

While a room-size rug is an ambitious undertaking, this smaller version can provide you with a family keepsake in much less time.

Rag rugs are inexpensive to make because you can use almost any fabric.

(For this example, we used old curtains and worn blue jeans.)

To get started, plan your colors in advance. You can use bright, dark, or neutral colors, or even a patterned fabric as we did here. The only requirement is that all the fabric you use have the same wash requirements, since you don't want the rug to shrink after laundering.

Also, the fabrics you use should be medium to heavy weight and densely woven to provide durability.

Cut your fabric strips between 1 and 3 inches in width, depending on the weight of the fabric. (Lighter-weight fabric can be cut wide; heavier fabric, such as the jeans material we used, works best in strips about 1½

inches wide.)

Turning what you have into something new and decorative makes you feel good. After all, recycling is nothing new. Grandma did it all the time.

Preparing the Strips

Before you begin braiding, you'll need to prepare several, if not all, of the strips you are going to use for the rug.

If you're using lightweight fabric, you may be able to tear this into 3-inch-wide strips. With heavier-weight fabrics, you will have to cut your strips with a scissors or rotary cutting tool and mat.

For this rug, we cut the patterned fabric in 1¾-inch widths; the ivory fabric at 2½-inch widths, and the blue jean fabric at 1½-inch widths.

Cut with the grain.

Size of your Rug

For an oval rug, your beginning braid length before the turn is generally ⅓ the size you want the rug to measure lengthwise when it's complete. For our 3-foot rug, we started with a 1-foot braid length. (Fig. 1)

Figure 1

SPECIAL PROJECT TIP

• If you are making a rag rug from used clothing such as jeans, make sure you avoid any worn through areas or pieces of fabrics with holes. You'll find that old wool clothing makes excellent (and authentic) rag rugs.

a

1 To start the braid, join two patterned strips with a bias seam. Before joining, insert a folded-down ivory strip. Iron to hold folds in place.

Sew bias seams diagonally across two strips that have been placed at right angles to each other with right sides together. Trim seam allowance to ⅛ inch. Roll up strips and secure with rubber band or clothespin.

Cross your right strip over your middle strips and then cross the left strip over the strip now in the middle. (If you've ever braided hair, the technique is the same.)

Continue braiding, pulling the fabric snug. If you need more tension, you can sew a piece of cord to the top of your braid and tie it to a doorknob or lay the braid on the table and weigh it down with a heavy book.

2 As you braid, fold in both edges and then fold in half so that no raw edges show (see Fig. 2). This way your rug is reversible and wears longer.

Keep the tension the same as you braid, and keep the fold line to the middle or back of the braid so it doesn't show.

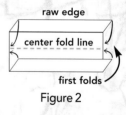

raw edge

center fold line

first folds

Figure 2

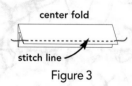

center fold

stitch line

Figure 3

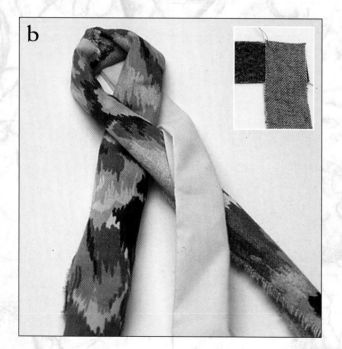

b

SPECIAL PROJECT TIP

• In this project, we added strips as we went and folded in our raw edges as we braided. As an alternative, you can sew several strips together, fold them down, and stitch close to the fold line (see Fig. 3). Keep in mind that it is easier to braid if you have less material to move around as you are braiding.

3 Add strips as you need them and watch your rug develop. Change color whenever you think it's needed; be sure to complete rings all the way around the rug for a pleasing look.

4 Lace the braid together on a flat surface to avoid warping. For this rug, the beginning center braid length was about 12 inches. Turn the braid length back on itself and start lacing it together with the carpet thread and large blunt needle. Lace outside loops to outside loops, skipping a stitch in between.

Pull the lacing snug but not too tight, to avoid creating a hump in your rug. Keep checking your rug as you go to make sure it remains flat. If a little curl develops, you can steam press the rug with a hot iron and a damp cloth.

5 To finish the rug as you approach the ending point, cut the strips slightly narrower so the last braid simply fades into a very narrow one. Tack it closely to the edge of the rug. Fold under any raw edges and tack down.

A Faux Stone *Plaque*

This attractive kitchen decor item mimics expensive architectural details in a lightweight form.

Tuscan- and Mediterranean-inspired rooms often make use of unique architectural forms as art. It may be a part of a stone column or a chipped piece of a plaster frieze, displayed as an object of beauty in a room.

We took this same idea and found a way to create our own unique art form that mimics the age-old look of these details.

We shaped, covered, sanded, and painted lightweight foam forms and joint compound into a faux stone sculpture.

We chose pears as our motif, but this technique works with any foam form you can find.

1 Using your serrated knife, cut foam eggs in half lengthwise. (Only three egg halves will be used.) Cut the top ½ inch off one egg, and use marker to place marks around egg, 1½ inches from the top. Create a second line 2½ inches from the top of the egg.

Using a scrap piece of foam as an abrasive, rub between the marked lines to start sanding the foam away on the egg. Angle sanding foam toward 1½-inch line to create a deeper groove along that line. When it is complete, the groove should be about ⅜ inch deep at the deepest point.

Continue sanding until foam begins to take on the rounded form of a pear. Sand along bottom to flatten slightly. Sand to round from flattened area to sides. Sand small groove in top back of pear to mimic hollow for stem. Create shallow hollow on pear bottom.

To create stems, cut 1-inch foam strip, 2 inches long and ½ inch wide. Turn piece on side. Cut in half to create two rectangles. Discard one section.

Shape stems by rolling and pinching until pieces resemble pear stems.

SPECIAL PROJECT TIP

• One of the easiest ways to sand foam to size is by using another piece of foam as a rasp or file. You'll find that this gives you nice control over how much of the foam form you remove.

You Will Need

• Two 5⅞-by-3⅞ foam eggs (we used Styrofoam-brand eggs that we found at our local Michael's craft shop)
• One 1-inch thick sheet of 8-by-16-inch foam
• Black marker
• Joint compound (found at hardware stores and home centers)
• Adhesive for gluing foam (we used Hold the Foam brand)
• Craft paints in shades of our choice (for this piece, we used Americana brand Acrylic Paint in Antique White, True Ochre, French Vanilla, Light Buttermilk, and Raw Sienna)
• 1-inch paintbrush
• Ruler
• Serrated knife
• 220-grit sandpaper
• Water

2 Foam-sand backs of pears to make sure they are flat.

Set pears on 1-inch sheet of foam. Center left to right and top to bottom. (Use the picture shown here as a placement guide.) Trace around outside of pears. Break edges of 1-inch foam to form an irregular outline. Break off a little at a time. Press foam on edges to soften breaks. Don't remove or press in any foam inside pear outline. Glue pears to foam. Glue stems into hollows. Allow to dry for 6 hours.

3 Lightly brush any loose foam off plaque. Load your brush with joint compound and begin to brush compound back and forth across plaque, working it into the foam. (It will look bumpy.) Cover the front, pears, and sides of plaque with a layer of joint compound. Allow to dry. Apply compound to back. Allow to dry.

Once the joint compound has dried completely, use sandpaper to sand pears gently. Don't over-sand. There will be pits and valleys, yet pears should not feel rough to touch. If foam shows in an area ¼ inch or larger, recoat, allow to dry, and resand.

Paint pears and plaque Antique White.

Brush True Ochre paint over pears. This is translucent paint; brush on smoothly. Add a bit of water to paint to make painting easier.

Paint stems Raw Sienna.

Mix water and French Vanilla (1 part water to 4 parts paint), and brush translucent mixture over pears, stems, and plaque.

Mix water and Light Buttermilk (1-to-4), and, using very little paint on your brush, lightly brush pears to add highlights. Brush randomly on plaque to lighten. Brush on a second coat for highlights.

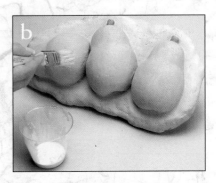

Autumn *Splendor*

This applique pillow design brings an ancient technique into the 21st century.

This fun technique uses appliqued felt flowers and leaves to create an attractive throw pillow. The design is further embellished with embroidery and a few glass beads for color.

This technique can also be adapted to a wide variety of other patterns, using the tricks shown here.

You Will Need

- ½ yard creme Dupioni silk
- Embroidery thread
- Wool felt in crimson, green, light brown and beige
- Glass beads
- 14-inch square pillow insert
- White and green sewing thread
- Tissue paper
- Embroidery and beading needles
- Mechanical pencil
- Tape
- Straight pins
- Scissors
- Sewing machine

Getting Started

Use a copier to enlarge the pattern at right by 245 percent. (If your enlargement requires using two pieces of paper, match the design and tape the papers together.)

Cutting Out the Pattern

The pattern indicates a letter (A, B, C, D) beside each leaf/flower. Each is labeled with the color felt for that section.

In cutting the felt, cut as close to the line as possible to maintain the shape of the applique. Use a pair of small sharp scissors to cut out the felt shapes.

Using the enlarged pattern and a thin-leaded mechanical pencil, trace the design on a piece of smooth tissue paper. (This tissue-paper pattern will be used later.) **TIP:** If necessary, iron the tissue paper with a warm iron to press it flat.

Using the enlarged pattern, cut out the paper patterns as follows:

Leaves A1, A2, and A3: Cut out all three pattern pieces; they vary in size. Mark on the pattern piece A1, A2, or A3 to remember where to place them.

Leave the pattern pinned to the appliqué until you are ready to use that leaf.

Flower B: Cut the petals in three pieces, following the lines between the colors.

Flower C: Cut as one piece. (A blanket stitch will later separate the petals.)

Flower D: Cut the petals as one piece. Cut the base and center along lines between colors.

Applique Pattern

Enlarge at 245%

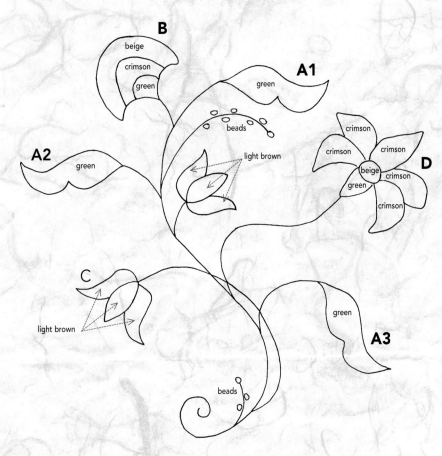

How to work the Stem Stitch

Place a small knot in the end of the thread. Always keep the thread on the downward side of the needle, working the stem stitch along the line.

Bring the needle up at 1 and down at 2. Bring needle up at 3, halfway between 1 and 2. Continue in this manner until area is completed.

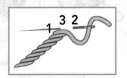

Figure 1

How to work the Blanket Stitch

Place a knot in the end of your thread, starting on the left side of the area. Bring the needle up at starting point as indicated at 1, hold the thread down with your thumb, and take the needle over (about ⅛ inch) and up (about ⅛ inch) to 2, going down at 2 and coming up at 3 (which is a new 1), keeping the thread under the needle at all times. Go up and over to 4 (same as 2), taking the needle down at 4, coming up at 5.

Continue in this manner until all stitches are in place.

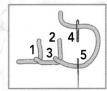

Figure 2

1 Cut out the felt following the color labeling on each of the paper pattern pieces. Cut two pieces of silk 13 inches square.

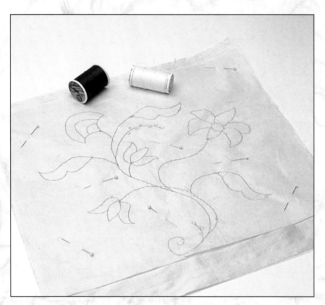

2 Center the tissue-paper-traced design on one piece of silk. Use white sewing thread and basting stitches to outline stems. Baste the leaves/flowers slightly inside the lines. For flowers C and D, baste only the outside edge. These basting lines will not show when the felt pieces are in place but work as guidelines for placing them. Use white sewing thread to baste the inside lines of the petals on the felt pieces for flowers C and D. (To make it easier to remove the basting threads for flowers C and D, place the basting knot on top of the felt.)

Use green sewing thread and small basting stitches to baste the stems onto the silk fabric. (As you stitch the stems next, you will cover these stitches so you won't need to remove the basting thread.) When basting is complete, remove the tissue paper.

Use three strands of dark green embroidery thread and the stem stitch (Fig. 1, page 33), to work the stems on the silk following the basting lines. Be careful that the silk does not pucker.

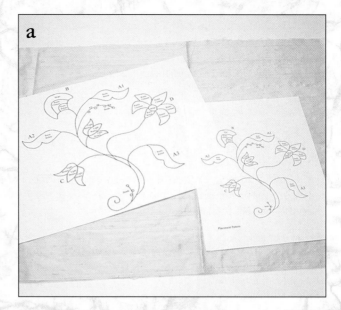
a

3 As you begin to pin the felt pieces in place on the silk fabric, refer back to your original pattern from time to time to keep the overall design in mind.

Use two strands of dark gold embroidery thread and the blanket stitch (Fig. 2, page 33) to stitch the felt onto the silk. Start blanket stitching the leaves, beginning with leaf A1. Start on the bottom left side of the leaf. Work leaves A2 and A3 in the same manner.

Start blanket stitching the flowers, beginning with flower B (3 pieces). Using the beige applique, start on the left side, stitching along the top edge. Be sure this piece is centered over the basting lines. NOTE: Side edges are stitched last on flower B.

b

Pin the crimson felt next to the beige, barely overlapping the beige. Stitch along the top edge, joining the beige and crimson pieces. Pin the green felt next to the crimson, barely overlapping and centered slightly over the stem stitch. Stitch along the top edge. Stitch the bottom starting on the left and working across the edge to the right side, connecting to the beige outside edge.

NOTE: The center petal is stitched last for flowers C and D. Using the blanket stitch, work flower C (one piece). Center flower C slightly over the stem stitch. Stitch the beige felt to the silk, turning the fabric so that you start your stitch-

ing on the right outside petal next to the center petal. Stitch across the top of the petal, down the side, across the bottom, and up the other side, ending next to the center petal.

Now work the inside center petal, removing the basting lines as you work. Always work from left to right. Work the other flower C in the same manner. Using the blanket stitch, work flower D. Stitch the crimson to the silk. Do not stitch along the inside edge of the flower petals where the beige felt will be attached. Turn the fabric so that you start next to the base area/green section of the flower. Work to the right around the outside of the two lower petals on either side of the center petal.

When the side petals are complete, work the center petal, removing the basting lines as you stitch. Center the green felt over the tip of the stem stitch. Stitch the two sides, leaving the top unstitched. Center the beige felt over the edge of the crimson and the green.

NOTE: If the beige piece does not completely cover all the unstitched area, you will need to cut another piece that is slightly larger. When the piece is centered, stitch around the area joining all the pieces.

4 Using two strands of thread that match the silk fabric, attach the beads as indicated on the pattern. Sew through each bead twice. Using a ½-inch seam allowance, sew the front of the pillow top to back, right sides together, leaving a 9-inch opening in the center of the bottom seam.

Insert the pillow form and slipstitch the opening closed.

SPECIAL PROJECT TIP

• With the blanket stitch, always work left to right, keeping the loop of thread under the needle as you work. Your other thumb is a key part of this stitch. Hold the thread with your other thumb so that the thread can always be under the needle. Keep the stitch length about ⅛ inch for both the vertical (straight) and horizontal (loop) parts of the stitch. If possible, place a blanket stitch on the pointed tip of the appliqué pieces to maintain the shape and to secure.

Natural *Beauty*

Nature inspires creativity, displaying its pure beauty in rich layers of simplicity and complexity. Discover how to weave natural elements into your home—indoors as well as your outdoor living space.

Enjoy time outside on a comfortable picnic table cushion that's easy to make yourself. Transform your home's entryway into a beautiful outdoor foyer with elements from nature's seasonal bounty. Add color and charm to a plain garden tote with rubber stamps in floral designs. Spotlight indoor flowers and plants with beautiful, uniquely crafted containers. You may just find yourself "shopping" for craft materials in your own backyard!

Decoupage Flower Plate

Make this pretty plate with dried flowers from your own garden, or with flowers purchased from the craft store.

Any size glass plate can be used for this project. We used an 8-inch dessert plate, but a dinner plate or serving platter can be beautiful too.

Dried flowers are very delicate, so working with a tweezers is helpful. You will be working on the bottom of the plate, not on the serving surface.

Remember to turn the flowers upside down on the bottom of the plate so the pretty "front" of the dried flower is what you see when you look at the plate. Some flowers are bulky and don't work well for this project, especially for the very bottom of the plate where it has to sit on the table. Choose the flattest flowers possible

when you're working on the bottom of the plate. Adding some greens and smaller flowers such as baby's breath gives the plate an airier look.

This plate is not dishwasher safe, so remember to hand wash only the top of the plate with the least amount of water possible.

You Will Need

- Clear glass plate
- White scrap paper
- Dried flowers and greens, purchased or home-dried
- Decoupage medium
- 8- by 10-inch sheet of mulberry paper, from craft or art store
- Sponge brush
- Sharp mat knife
- Tweezers

2 Turn plate over and paint one coat of decoupage medium on the bottom third of the bottom of the plate. Use tweezers to transfer dried flowers from your sample circle to bottom of plate. Remember to turn flowers so the "front" of each flower is facing up. Continue adding decoupage medium, one-third at a time; let dry. Apply two additional coats of the decoupage solution to seal flowers on plate; let dry between each coat for at least an hour.

1 Remove all labels and wash plate thoroughly with soap and water. Trace around your plate and cut a circle of paper the same size as your plate on a piece of white scrap paper. Arrange flowers on circle of paper the way you will want them to be placed on the plate. Set plate on top of circle and dried flowers to get an idea of how your finished plate will look.

3 Tear one sheet of mulberry paper into small, irregular pieces, about 2 by 2 inches. Apply one coat of decoupage medium to the bottom of the plate. Adhere torn mulberry paper to back of plate. (This will seal the bottom of the plate and has a nice, transparent look.) Let dry. Apply one more coat to seal all. Turn plate upside down and use a very sharp knife to cut excess mulberry paper away from the rim of the plate.

Decoupage Flower Plate   **39**

A Garden *Spindle*

Support your plants in style with a decorative, sun-catching garden spindle.

This garden project has endless possibilities: different spindles, different finials, different paint, different beads—so many options!

Using only items from your local home improvement and craft stores—or even items you have around the house—you can create decorative plant supports, or just a piece of garden art with a bit of whimsy. (Consider: Spindles can be bought new or found at a salvage yard. The finials can be off old drapery rods or a bedpost, or purchased in the unpainted wood section of your craft store.)

Whether you have a cottage garden or a formal garden, you'll surely find a perfect spot for a garden spindle.

You Will Need

- Tapered wood deck or stair spindle
- Saw
- Wood finial
- Drill and drill bit
- 2-inch dowel screw
- Needle-nosed pliers
- Wood glue
- Weatherproof acrylic paint (we used a brand called Patio Paint)
- Weatherproof acrylic clear coat
- 18-gauge copper wire
- Assorted beads with holes large enough to fit on 18-gauge wire

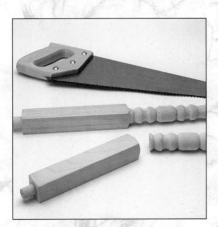

1 Using a hand saw, remove the top, square portion of your wooden spindle.

SPECIAL PROJECT TIP

- When you thread beads onto your wire, mix the textures and shapes. Pair frosted beads with sparkling beads, and round beads with square beads. Different shapes make the piece more interesting.

2 Mark a center point at the top of the wooden spindle and the bottom of the finial. Drill pilot holes for the dowel screws. Twist dowel screw into finial, holding screw portion with a pair of pliers. Stop at the halfway point of the dowel screw. Spread wood glue on top of spindle and twist wood spindle onto dowel screw until finial and wood spindle come together. Wipe off excess glue and let dry.

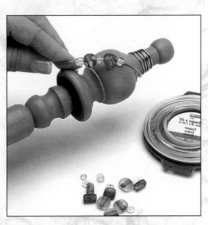

4 Cut about 3 feet of 18-gauge copper wire. Using a needle-nosed pliers, bend back one end of the copper wire to form a small loop. Start wrapping wire around the top of the finial. We wrapped the wire around our finial five times. String a couple of beads on the wire at this point and stretch the wire over the ball in the finial. Continue wrapping wire around base of finial. Using the needle-nosed pliers, form a small loop at the end of the wire and cut off excess.

3 Paint garden spindle with two coats of weatherproof acrylic paint and one coat of clear coat. Allow paint to dry between coats.

5 Cut another 4 feet or so of 18-gauge copper wire. Using the needle-nosed pliers, as in previous step, bend wire to form a small loop. Wrap wire around three times at the top of spindle just under finial. Thread approximately 8 inches of beads onto the wire and continue to wrap them around the spindle. Add more beads and continue wrapping to desired length. Finish by wrapping wire three times around the spindle. Cut off excess wire and form a small loop with a needle-nosed pliers at end of wire.

A Garden Spindle

Art in the Garden

Add some sparkle to the garden with this clever, easy-to-make mosaic wind chime that will catch every ray of sunshine.

Motion in the garden can be very subtle. Leaves tremble, ornamental grasses sway, and light dances around the yard. You can add to this sense of movement by making this charming mobile for your garden.

Hang this mobile in a tree or under the eaves on your house and enjoy the light show that the twisting and turning mirrors and mosaic pieces provide. If you use weatherproof paint and waterproof glue, this mobile will withstand the outdoor elements beau-tifully. (You may even have many of the supplies needed for this project around the house left over from previous projects.)

You Will Need

- One ⅞-inch wood dowel rod
- Two 1⅝-inch large wood candle cups
- Wood glue
- Weatherproof acrylic paint (we used a brand called Patio Paint)
- Weatherproof acrylic clear coat (Patio Paint)
- Seven 9/16-inch screw eyes
- Chain to hang mobile
- Transparent fishing line
- Glass mosaic tiles
- Decorative glass shapes
- Accent and designer marbles
- Square mirrors in assorted sizes
- Round mirrors in assorted sizes
- Silver beads
- Clear epoxy

1 Using a hand saw or power miter saw, cut a piece of wood dowel 12 inches long. Glue large candle cups onto both ends of dowel rod. Paint dowel rod with two coats of weatherproof paint in a color of your choice, and finish with one coat of clear coat.

2 To mark the placement of the screw eyes that you will use to hang the streamers, measure in 1 inch from each side of the wood dowel. Screw in screw eyes. (You may want to predrill holes where marked to make this step easier.) Evenly space the three remaining screw eyes between the two end eyes. (We placed our screw eyes about every 2 inches on our dowel.)

To hang the mobile, add two additional screw eyes on top of the candle cups. Using a pliers to open links on your chain, attach the chain to the two end screw eyes.

4 Cut a length of fishing line about 3 feet long and fold it in half. With the fishing line sandwiched between your mobile pieces, glue matching mosaic and mirror pieces back to back, using 2-part epoxy according to manufacturer's directions.

3 For the most pleasing effect, you'll want to consider the size and shapes of the various mosaic and mirror pieces you'll use on your streamers. We found the easiest way to do this was to lay out our different pieces as they would appear on our mobile and shift them until we were happy with the placement.

5 To attach mosaic streamers to screw eyes, insert fishing line through hole and twist the end around the fishing line two times. Secure line by bringing end through loop and pulling tight.

Cut off excess line.

American *Style*

This super-simple painting project lets you turn an inexpensive wood crate into a vintage American flag container.

Storage with style is a goal for any homeowner. That's why finding cute, clever ways to create more storage options can be such a rewarding project.

We found a way to turn an unpainted wooden crate into a delightful container that will work well as an accent in your room or, as we have done here, as a decorative way to display plants on a deck.

This entire project cost about $20, but you can make multiples of this flag box for very little extra expense once you've purchased your paint and other supplies.

1 Spray the entire box, inside and out, with red spray paint. We found it worked best to spray the inside of the box first, let that dry, then spray the outside of the box. Apply several light coats for the best finish.

When the red base coat is dry, use painter's tape to mask off alternate stripes on the box and to cover the upper left corner completely. (When you apply the tape for the stripes, look at the overall dimensions of the box and space stripes accordingly. You'll need to account for the spaces between the box slats as you apply the tape to give your flag a proper dimension.)

2 After applying tape, crumple some newspaper and set it loosely inside the box to keep the paint in the next step from bleeding through the back and sides of the box. Spray the front of the box, over the tape, with several light coats of white spray paint. Let dry.

When the paint has dried, remove the tape to reveal alternating red and white stripes.

3 Either mask off the background star section of the flag and use blue spray paint on this section, or use an artist's brush and craft paint to fill in this area. Let dry completely.

4 Using a fine-tipped artist's brush and white craft paint, add stars to the blue background. (Draw your five-point stars by starting at the left of the arm and pulling the brush right to the opposite point, drawing the brush down to form the lower left leg, and then crossing up to the top and down to finish. This is the same way you drew stars as a child.) Placing the stars randomly looks more natural than rigid rows and will give the box a vintage country feel.

5 When the piece has dried completely, place three or four drops of brown craft paint on a paper plate. Add about two tablespoons of clear acrylic glaze and mix well.

Use a soft cloth to dip up a bit of the brown glaze and rub it into the front of the box, moving in small circles. Apply glaze until the box has achieved an antiqued patina. Wipe off excess and let dry.

As a final step, apply several coats of a protective polyurethane to the outside and inside of the box to seal the piece.

Perfect *Pots*

Dressing up plain terra cotta pots will make the outside of your containers as charming as the flowers inside.

Chunky terra cotta pots have a charm all their own, but sometimes these useful little garden foot soldiers can seem a bit dull when they're lined up on a deck or on a front stoop. There are several ways you can up the decorative value of these pots. Here are just a few quick suggestions that can jump-start a beautiful garden.

Using Stencils on Terra Cotta

The scope and variety of ready-made stencils on the market is astonishing. You can find botanical images and flowers, as well as almost any other decoration you can imagine. However, applying a flat stencil to a steadily curved surface, as on a pot, can be difficult. You'll find that even if you use a spray adhesive to place your stencil, you cannot satisfactorily paint through the design since there will be gaps that allow the paint to smudge through.

There's an easy way to remedy this. Simply place the stencil against your pot and use a pencil to transfer the image to the surface a bit at a time. You can adjust the stencil's position as you go, leaving a mirror image of the stencil on the pot. To paint our stenciled design directly on the pot, we used a specialty paint marker by Uchida designed for use on terra cotta. After we had colored the design to our satisfaction, we let it dry, and then used a permanent marker to outline the image, which let us hide any small imperfections along the edges.

SPECIAL PROJECT TIP

• You can use a wide variety of items to create personalized pots. Consider stencils, specialty paints, ribbons, raffia, or even small glass stones or mosaic materials to add style to your containers. One trick for getting a nice finished result when you're decorating terra cotta is to first spray the piece, inside and out, with a sealer. Since terra cotta is naturally porous, sealing the pot will prevent water from "leaking" through and affecting your designs.

It's also a good idea to use a second container inside the outer pot to further protect your artwork from dirt and water. You can finish all of these pots by adding a final coat of sealant to the outside, which will help protect your designs from the weather.

Add Texture to Your Pots

Decorative textured pots can cost big bucks at an elegant garden store. You can mimic the look for pennies using specialty paint and your trusty glue gun.

We sealed the pot with terra cotta sealer and let it dry. We then used X-Metals, a specialty paint made by Krylon, to paint our entire pot in a metallic purple shade with several light coats. Once the pot was dry, we turned it upside down and used a glue gun to apply thick strands of glue on the pot. You can make a geometric pattern or create a random effect, as we did.

Once the glue has hardened, apply several more coats of spray paint over the glue. The glue will take on a unique, reflective appearance loaded with eye-appeal. (Water can loosen hot glue, so be sure to use this pot with a separate inner container. It's also a good idea to use it in a sheltered spot.)

Classic Pinstripes

This is one of the fastest—and easiest!—ways to add a little class to your pots. Simply spray the pots with a terra cotta sealer, let dry, and then paint the entire pot a base color using spray paint in your choice of shade. (We painted our pot bright yellow.) Then grab a handful of rubber bands in a variety of widths and place them around your pot. You can arrange the rubber bands in smooth, even lines, or you can let them make a random shape around the pot. Once the bands are in place, spray the entire pot with a second, contrasting shade of spray paint. (We chose a deep blue.) Let the pot dry completely, then remove the rubber bands. You'll have a unique pinstriped pot.

A Window Box Table

Turn an inexpensive wooden window box into a clever storage space, perfect for use in a foyer.

This project makes use of a premade wooden window box that we purchased at our local home improvement store for about $20. The piece is 28 inches long and about 7 inches tall. It is designed for use on decks or mounted outside windows as a place to plant flowers.

We liked the look of this piece and thought we'd bring the outdoors inside by adding inexpensive wood spindle legs to the box to create a catchall for use in a foyer. (We paired the finished piece with an old window that we took to our local hardware store, where we had the glass panes replaced with mirror.)

Getting Started

Sand any rough edges on your window box and use wood filler to fill in any nail head or staple holes. The sanding doesn't have to be perfect, but you don't want any rough splinters exposed. Prime spindles and window box using a good quality primer paint designed for use on wood.

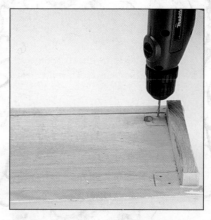

1 We wanted our box table to be about 32 inches high once we attached the legs. Our wooden spindles were about 37 inches tall and square on each end. To accommodate our planned table height, we cut about 6 inches off each end of each spindle, saving the scrap wood we removed.

Sand any rough edges after cutting.

NOTE: When cutting spindles, it is important to have a straight cut so that the finished table will be level. Use a miter box or power miter saw to keep your cuts straight.

Trace the leg placement in the corners on the bottom of the window box.

2 Pre-drill two holes inside the markings for each of the leg placements. Working from the inside of the window box, attach the legs using 1½-inch drywall screws.

SPECIAL PROJECT TIP

• For good balance, it is important to be sure that the legs are straight on your table. Check this by using a small level at the top of the legs.

3 You'll need a small brace at the bottom of the legs to keep them straight. Measure the distance between the top of the legs along the side of the window box. Cut two pieces equal to this measurement from the scrap pieces of the spindles.

4 Place the window box upside down on your work surface. Mark the placement for the brace on the outside of each leg. Pre-drill and countersink holes. Attach the brace using 2-inch drywall screws. Fill screw heads with wood filler, let dry, and sand smooth.

Finish the project with two coats of paint and a coat of protective polyurethane spray.

You can fill this window box table with plants for a fresh spring/summer look and make it a catchall for gloves and mittens in the winter.

You Will Need

- Wooden window box
- Four wooden spindles
- Wood filler and spatula
- 180-grit sandpaper
- Primer
- Paintbrush
- Measuring tape
- Miter box and saw
- Drill, drill bit, and countersink bit
- Drywall screws—1½- and 2-inch
- Small level
- Screwdriver
- Paint
- Polyurethane

5 minutes and Fabulous

Check out these extra-quick ways to add a little spark to an inexpensive garden bouquet!

Behold the humble glass vase. You can buy these for pennies at any craft, garden, or gift store, and they are inexpensive enough to give as a hostess gift filled with garden flowers every time you make a visit in the summer.

Unfortunately, these little workhorses don't have much flair. They do their job, but they don't do it with any real style.

You can personalize these little dears in (about) five minutes to match whatever blooms you care to display. These adornments are cheap, they're easy, and, best of all, they'll bring smiles to the faces of those who see them.

Outstanding Oriental Display

This one just couldn't be simpler. Wrap a bamboo place mat around your glass vase, and secure it with double-sided tape. This is an especially elegant trick paired with a spare but lovely arrangement of flowers with a Japanese flavor.

It's a Party

Finding ways to use up the bits and pieces of leftover craft material around the house is always a pleasure. This festive little container is adorned with nothing more than a twirl of leftover paper ribbon from Christmas. Simply use a piece of double-stick tape on the base of your vase, anchor one end of the ribbon there, and then twirl it around the vase until it looks like a barber's pole. Simple, fun, and festive.

Delicate and Delightful

Wide (2-inch) wired ribbon is a terrific item to have around the house. It makes lovely bows to top impromptu presents and it adds a bit of spice to dried flower swags and other decorative accessories.

You can also turn wire ribbon into a fanciful little skirt to curl around the bottom of a vase. Simply select a piece with colors that complement your blooms and cut off a section about 6 feet long. Expose the wires on each side of one end of the ribbon and begin pulling. As you pull, the ribbon will curl and gather itself into a pouffy circle. Once you've gathered the ribbon as much as you like, tuck it around the base of the vase and pinch the ends together to keep it in place. Finish off your display by tucking a few inexpensive glass marbles around the stems.

Raffish Raffia

Even a blowzy bunch of the simplest garden posies looks delightful in a vase wrapped with raffia. Wrap and tie the ribbons of raffia around the vase, securing everything with a bow. You can even tuck a spare flower inside the bow for a fleeting—but lovely—bit of whimsy.

Shiny and Splendid

If you really want an elegant arrangement, nothing beats dressing up a plain glass vase with a spritz or two of Krylon's Looking Glass spray paint. This beautiful mirror-finish paint can make even the cheapest vase look stunning. For this arrangement, we sprayed the inside of our vase with a very light coat of the paint and then added just a tiny spritz of a purple metallic spray paint to the outside to match our purple statice arrangement.

A Picnic Bench Cushion

Relax in comfort as you celebrate the fleeting days of summer.

Summertime means backyard bar-becues, and this nifty project will ensure that your guests linger at the picnic table in comfort.

This simple box cushion is designed to fit on a picnic table bench and is attached with fabric ties, which means you can take your cushions with you to a public park or even on vacation.

You Will Need

- 5½ yards fabric for two cushions
- 2-inch high-density foam (often sold in 24-by-75-inch sheets)
- Two zippers (we used 24-inch)
- Marker and yardstick
- Utility knife
- Measuring tape
- Scissors
- Iron

A 4" by 20"— cut 8

B 3" by 13"— cut 4

C 2" by 73"— cut 4

D 3" by 73"— cut 2

E 13" by 73"— cut 4

(The finished size of these cushions will be 12 by 72 inches. If your table is a different size, you'll need to adjust your cut sizes.)

1 CUTTING THE FABRIC FOR THE TWO BOX CUSHIONS: The E sections will be the top and bottom of your cushions. The D section will be one side, and C will be the zippered side. B is the ends of your cushion, and A will form the ties.

2 Measure and cut foam to desired width and length. TIP: Place a yard-stick along your markings and use it as a guide as you cut through your foam. The yardstick will help keep your cut-ting lines straight.

3 MAKING THE TIES: Using fabric strips A, fold in raw edge along one short end ½ inch and press. Fold fabric in half lengthwise, right side out, and press. Open and fold each raw edge in toward center crease line and press. Fold fabric in half lengthwise again and press. All raw edges should now be concealed except the short end of the tie, which will be concealed when it is sewn into the seam.

4 INSTALLING THE ZIPPER: Sew the 2-by-73-inch B strips of fabric together using ½-inch seam allowance. Press seam open. Fold fabric strip and zipper in half and mark center with a pin. Center zipper on strip of fabric right side down; zipper teeth should also be centered in seam allowance. Pin in place. Install zipper foot on sewing machine. Topstitch zipper in place, sewing across tape at closed end of the zipper. Use seam ripper to open seam over zipper.

5 FINISHING THE CUSHION: Sew fabric strips B, C, and D together to form a band for the box cushion using ½-inch seam allowance. Mark center of side strips with a pin. Fold fabric piece E in half lengthwise. Mark the center on each side with a pin. Place top of cushion E right side up on your work surface. Right sides together, pin band to cushion top, lining up raw edges and center pin markings. Sew in place using ½-inch seam allowance.

6 Pin ties in place about 10 inches in from outside edges on both sides at both ends of cushion. Sew in using ⅜-inch seam allowance. Reinforce stitch-ing to ensure ties are very secure. Open zipper and attach bottom of cushion as described in Step 5. Turn cushion right side out and insert foam.

The Luminous *Pumpkin*

This simple technique lets you turn a run-of-the-mill pumpkin into a piece of holiday art!

Many of us consider fall to be our favorite season—when the leaves begin to change into their magical rainbow of colors and the air brings a crisp chill.

Fall signals the beginning of the harvest, a wonderful time to celebrate the season with some extra-special treats, like the beautifully carved pumpkins shown here.

Pumpkin carving, the fall season's most popular activity for young and old alike, can be an art form.

The pumpkin-carving techniques here use a relief-style technique that produces an easy yet elegant design on the outer skin of the pumpkin. The tools required are simple, and the method doesn't take any longer than making a standard jack-o'-lantern. This effect is far prettier, and you're sure to wow friends and family with your efforts.

You can use this technique either to make a vase for fall flowers or to create a spot for a candle to illuminate the inside of the pumpkin.

You Will Need

- Pumpkin
- Fresh leaves (for a template)
- Masking tape
- Craft knife
- Wood chisel
- Linoleum cutter (you can find these at your local hardware store)
- Large spoon or ice cream scoop
- Paper towels

SPECIAL PROJECT TIP

• If while carving you "slip" with the wood chisel and carve off a portion of the design, you can use a product called Zap-A-Gap to glue the piece of pumpkin in place. Zap-A-Gap (also called CA-7) is a waterproof "super glue" that works well on moist pumpkin skin. You can buy it at most hobby stores where supplies for model-making can be found.

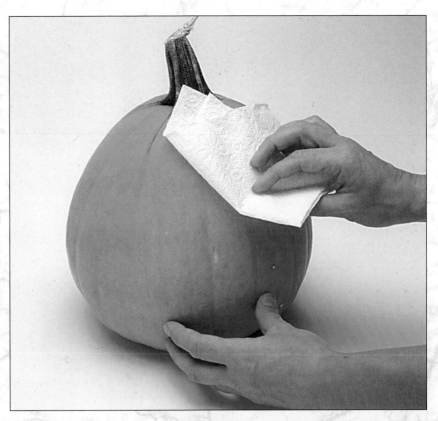

1 Choose a pumpkin that has a fairly smooth surface free from blemishes. A clean, dry surface ensures that tape will stick. Wipe the surface of the pumpkin with paper towels to remove any excess moisture and all dirt.

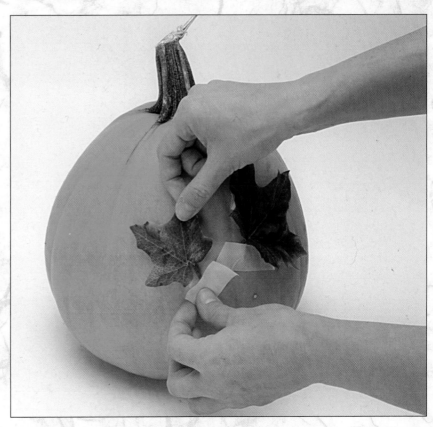

2 Using masking tape, decoratively arrange and then securely tape two or three fall leaves (from trees, shrubs, or flowers) on the front of the pumpkin. You can use leaves that are the same or arrange different leaves to create the design you want.

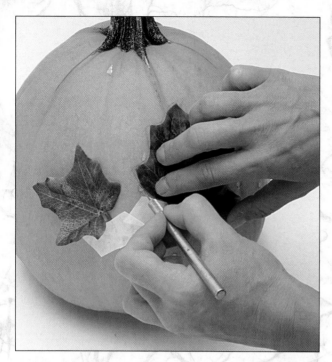

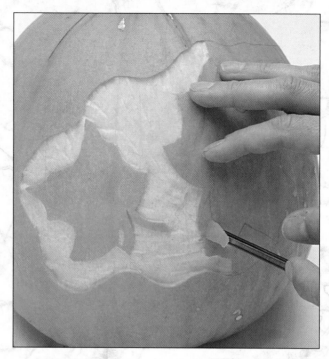

3 Using a craft knife, trace the outside edges of the leaves, cutting about ⅛ to ¼ inch into the skin of the pumpkin.

Remove the tape and leaves. Further frame the central leaf designs by using your craft knife to carve one freehand scalloped border around the outline of the carved leaves to frame them. (Think of this as a picture frame for the central design.)

4 Using a wood chisel, gently carve away all the pumpkin skin between the leaf design and the border to expose the leaves.

Apply only a small amount of pressure to remove the skin. Be careful to take away only small portions at a time so you do not accidentally remove the leaf design.

(Any size wood chisel works, but a smaller one with a ¼ - inch blade works best. Wood chisels are available at most hardware stores.)

NOTE: When using the wood chisel and the linoleum cutter in the following step, it is easiest (and safest) to carve away from yourself as you carve the design.

5 Using the linoleum cutter, gently cut veinlike lines into the leaves to give them a more realistic look.

6 With a paring knife, remove the top of the pumpkin by making zigzag cuts around the top.

Carefully and gently remove the top in one piece. Remove the stringy flesh and seeds from the inside of the pumpkin using a spoon or ice cream scoop.

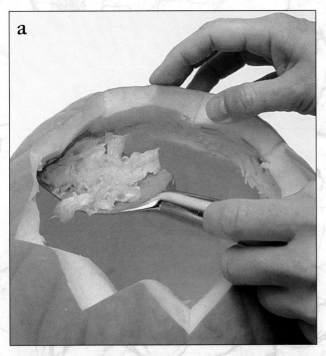

a

7 If you plan to use your pumpkin as a vase, you can skip Steps 8 and 9. Simply place a piece of florist's foam inside the cavity of the pumpkin (b), add about four inches of water, and arrange your flowers inside. If you plan to place a candle in your pumpkin, continue as follows:

Again, using the spoon or ice cream paddle (a), remove extra flesh from the front of the pumpkin which holds the design, until the wall of the pumpkin becomes about ¼ inch thick.

(The thinner you can shave the wall of the pumpkin without breaking it, the easier it will be to see the candle when it is lit.)

8 Once the wall of the pumpkin is thin enough, use a paring knife to cut small quarter-sized crescent-shaped slits around the leaf design on the front of the pumpkin. This will let the light shine through when the candle is lit. Cut as many slits as you want on the front of the pumpkin. The more slits you cut, the more light will shine through when lit. Carve several holes in the lid as well, which will let in air and will help the candle stay lit.

9 Place a small pillar candle in the pumpkin and light it before displaying. If the pumpkin will be used outside on a windy evening, place the candle in a largemouth glass jar, such as a canning jar, before placing it inside the pumpkin to prevent the wind from blowing it out.

SPECIAL PROJECT TIP

• Place a thin layer of petroleum jelly on the carved portion of the pumpkin using a cotton swab to help seal in the pumpkin's natural moisture and extend the life of the carved pumpkin.

b

Rings of Nature

With a world of supplies at our fingertips, it's easy to forget that nature offers us beautiful materials for free.

Many of us love to admire the annual rings of a sawn tree trunk. We want to know how old the tree is, but we also simply like the beautiful, concentric design. Capture this mystery and beauty in your own home by cutting tree branches into thin slices and using them to make or decorate a variety of objects.

NOTE: This project is not particularly difficult, but it does take significant prep work to cut and sand the branch sections, and you'll need to let the pieces dry for about two weeks before starting to glue. Also, you'll need to select several similarly sized branches with which to start. See the Tip on the next page for suggestions.

You Will Need

- Branches with diameters of about 1¾ inches
- 100- and 150-grit sandpaper
- Masking tape
- Wood glue
- Disposable paintbrush
- Beeswax, butcher's wax, shellac, or varnish
- Small hammer
- Handsaw or chisel

Fruit Bowl

1 Cut 165 ³⁄₁₆-inch slices, plus a few extras, from your branches. Cut the branches using a sharp handsaw. A saw guide, such as the one shown, will make the job easier, faster, and safer. You may also use a band saw, if you have access to one.

Sand the pieces smooth, first with 100-grit sandpaper and then with 150-grit. The easiest way to sand is to tape the sandpaper to a work surface grit side up and to vigorously rub the slices against it. Let the pieces dry for about two weeks before proceeding.

2 Make a rectangular cardboard template following the dimensions shown below (A). Draw a diagonal line from the 4-inch center marks to the opposite corners to create your bowl shape. (You'll use this in the next step.) Arrange the first layer of branch slices as closely as possible within the pencil guides. (Do not glue them to the cardboard.) Glue the second layer of branch circles to the first with wood glue. Repeat for other three sides.

3 When the four sides are glued, cut out the pencil template and use it to trace the exact shape of the bowl sides on the glued slices. Cut away excess portions of slices with a sharp handsaw. As with any sawing project, try to cut slightly to the "waste" side of your cutting line.

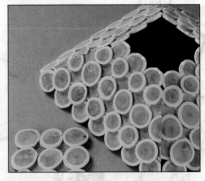

4 Arrange nine slices in a square. Glue four slices on top of them overlapping the pieces below to form the bottom. Let dry. Sand all surfaces smooth and prepare the sides for assembly by applying masking tape as shown.

5 Apply glue to all side joints with a disposable brush. Use the tape to hold the sides together as the glue dries. Be sure to wipe off glue drips before they dry so you won't have to sand them off later.

6 When the glue is dry, smooth the joints with sandpaper and glue the bottom on.

To finish the piece, apply beeswax with a piece of cloth or a brush and polish it afterwards. You many also finish the bowl with butcher's wax, shellac, or varnish.

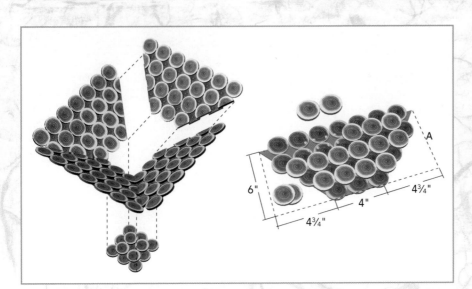

6"
4"
4³⁄₄"
4³⁄₄"
A

SPECIAL PROJECT TIP

• All sorts of tree branches can be used for these projects, but hardwood species work best. Maple, birch, and poplar are good candidates. There's no sticky sap to deal with and they are less apt to split or crack than many softwoods. Cut some sample branches to see how you like the color and ring patterns inside.

For these projects, we used laburnum branches. We removed the bark with a sharp knife (although this is optional) and allowed our slices to dry for two weeks at room temperature before beginning our projects.

Wine Caddy

You Will Need

- 2-inch-diameter branches
- ¼-inch plywood scraps (inexpensive plywood works fine)
- 3 pieces of 25-inch 12-gauge steel wire
- 12 ½-inch brads
- 3½ yards sisal string
- Mahogany wood stain
- Wood glue
- 100- and 150-grit sandpaper
- Small hammer
- Sharp handsaw or wood chisel
- Pliers with wire cutter

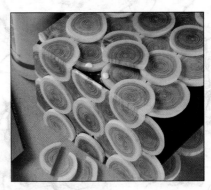

1 Cut 98 branch slices, plus some extras, $\frac{3}{16}$ inch thick and about 2 inches in diameter. (Follow Step 1 from Page 59 to prepare the slices.)

Cut three plywood pieces $3\frac{1}{2}$ by 6 inches; two pieces 6 by $8\frac{1}{4}$ inches and one piece 4 by $8\frac{1}{4}$ inches. (See illustration below right.)

Cut out $\frac{1}{8}$-inch-square notches for the handle in each side of the center B piece, one inch from the top edge. Glue and nail the sides (C) to the center partition and to the two end pieces (A). Then glue and nail on the bottom (D). When assembling small wood projects with nails, it's easier to start the nails while the work piece is lying on a flat surface as shown. Once the glue dries, sand lightly and stain the plywood box with a mahogany stain.

2 Glue the first layer of slices to the front and sides of the caddy with wood glue. Then glue the second layer on top of the first one, leaving the corners for last.

3 Cut slices to fit neatly together at the corners as shown. To do so, first test fit and mark your cut lines with a pencil. Then make the cuts with a sharp saw or a sharp wood chisel, and glue in place. Apply the finish of your choice to seal. (See Step 6 on Page 59.)

Dimensions for Wood Pieces

(see Step 1)

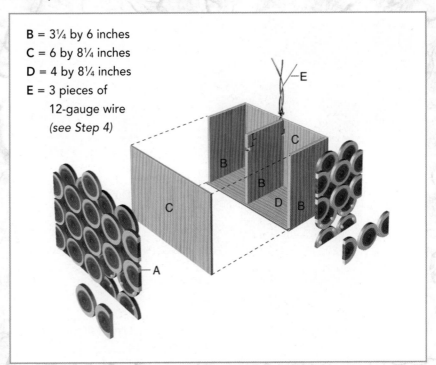

B = $3\frac{1}{4}$ by 6 inches
C = 6 by $8\frac{1}{4}$ inches
D = 4 by $8\frac{1}{4}$ inches
E = 3 pieces of
   12-gauge wire
(see Step 4)

4 Clamp the ends of three pieces of wire to a workbench. A small vise or even a C clamp will do. Loosely braid the handle wire. Then secure the ends to the partition notches by twisting. Cut off the excess. For a finished look, wind sisal twine around the handle top.

Dressed
for the *Season*

Create an entry for your home that welcomes all who visit.

When most people think of accessories, they think jewelry, scarves, shoes, or purses. But an accessory is really any little item that adds a pulled together look to an outfit—or in this case, to a home.

The homeowner at this attractive bungalow knows how to give her house a "dressed to impress" feeling for both fall and winter. She makes use of a variety of decorative pieces, massed to create a warm and welcoming impression.

You can take advantage of a few of her tips in your own home both this fall and winter.

Wonderful Window Boxes

Window boxes can be the ultimate home accessory. These "boxes" are actually wire frames that have been lined with coconut fiber, an absorbent material that holds water and encourages plant growth. Once you've pulled the season's last flowers, use the window box as a frame for all things fall.

This casually elegant display contains a wide variety of gourds—which will last for weeks in the cool temperatures of fall—mingled with random armloads of dried grass, wheat sheaves, and bundles of Indian corn with dried husks intact.

Window boxes aren't difficult to add to a home; visit your local home improvement store and you'll find dozens of ready-to-attach models that provide a perfect platform for creativity.

Captivating Color

Don't forget the impact a splash of color can have on an entry. This warm red screen door draws the eye, and a loose swag of grapevine curls around and down the sides to add a bit of whimsy. A collection of inexpensive mums in eye-popping colors have even more impact when several branches of curly willow are tucked inside, adding to the wispy, relaxed grouping. A couple pieces of galvanized tin sitting on the steps give the entry a classic country appeal.

Handsome Hooks

Don't put away those wrought-iron plant hangers quite yet. Instead, grab a child's jack-o'-lantern pumpkin pail; wrap the handle in a few strands of raffia, and tie it to one of the hooks. You can cradle a beautiful, unblemished real pumpkin in a sling made of simple rough twine on the second hanger, and place a decorative copper birdhouse on top of the shepherd's hook pole for balance.

Ribbons and Raffia

When the snow finally does fly later this year, don't let your doors feel underdressed. To meet the season in appropriate finery, select two colors of ribbon—one wide and one narrow. Layer the ribbons together, the smaller on top, and use removable tape to "wrap" your front door. Tie a bow in the center, and sneak a few strings of raffia through to make the whole presentation a little more relaxed.

Sprawling Spruce

Bundles of spruce tips are always a perfect winter window box staple, but don't line them up like little soldiers. Instead, let a few tip sideways and diagonally in a sprawl, and then use a collection of weatherproof holiday ornaments as decorative accents between and among the branches themselves. Add a grapevine wreath for even more mix-and-match delight.

Bright Birdhouses

Even if their tenants have flown south for the winter, decorative birdhouses are always a gorgeous accent item. These brightly colored houses, one with a festive raffia bow, line the edges of the front steps to add a cheery appearance.

A Painted Garden Tote

Use rubber stamps and bright metallic paints to make an adorable garden carryall.

H ave you ever wondered what it would be like to use your favorite rubber stamps to cre- ate a special design on fabric? In the project below, you can make a tote that will rival the blooms in your garden!

Getting Started

Prewash and dry tote bag, but do not use fabric softener. Iron tote flat. Line the inside of pockets (or areas you've chosen to paint) with freezer paper, waxed-side up. If the wax paper slips, iron lightly to keep it in place.

Tear tape lengthwise into strips long enough to form a frame. Place it on your fabric with the torn edge to the inside of your framed area. When you have a framed shape (square, rectangle, etc.), divide it into several smaller regions using the same torn tape technique. Be sure that you have torn edges on all exposed sides within the main frame. Press tape firmly into fabric, especially along the torn edges.

3 Using opaque black fabric paint, ink a small square of stamp foam. TIP: You may also use a dry ink pad and ink it yourself, or purchase a black fabric ink pad such as that made by Fabrico.

Lightly ink your stamps with the foam square, or from the inked pad. Be careful not to apply ink too thickly, or you will get blotches on your fabric.

Stamp images onto painted fabric and hold for a few seconds. For a more artistic look, let some of the images overlap the stripes of tape that frame your work area. (Be careful not to let your stamp extend past the outer border of tape.)

Fill in as much of your sponged area as you wish. TIP: You may want to slip a small cutting board or other firm, flat object under your stamping area to ensure a flat stamping surface.

1 Sponge a light coat of opaque white textile paint into the framed outline, being certain that paint goes to the edge of the torn tape. You want this layer to dry quickly, so apply only a light coat. If you apply the paint too heavily, the fabric will be stiff and you will have to wait to complete the project. You may dry with a hair dryer if necessary.

2 Beginning with your lightest color, sponge various shades of paint onto the primed area of tote one at a time. Apply colors randomly, and allow them to blend a little. Again, apply colors in thin layers for best results.

Allow this to dry to the touch.

You Will Need

- Canvas tote bag with pockets, suitable for garden tools
- Acrylic textile opaque fabric paints (we used Jacquard No. 123 white and No. 588 black)
- Acrylic textile colored and metallic fabric paints (we used Lumiere brands by Jacquard: No. 571 Pearl Turquoise, No. 141 Metallic Gold, No. 562 Metallic Olive Green, No. 564 Super Copper, No. 348 Metallic Violet)
- Cosmetic sponges, stamping sponges, or foam brushes
- 2-inch-square stamp pad foam (we used Cut n' Dry foam)
- Variety of rubber stamps
- Freezer wrap
- Painter's tape (2-inch works best)
- Latex or rubber gloves
- Paper towels
- Cutting board or other firm surface to slip inside pockets for support when stamping
- Iron and press cloth

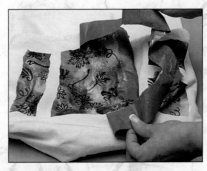

4 Allow image to dry about 10 minutes. Carefully pull off the tape to reveal the image below. Set tote aside to dry for 24 hours and then remove freezer paper from inside the tote.

5 To set your image, iron from both sides for 30 seconds using a blotting cloth so that the iron doesn't come into direct contact with the paint. The tote is now washable.

Mementos & Gifts

We all like to ferret away little pieces of our past in drawers or boxes—small, meaningful treasures that we just can't bear to part with. And that's fine! Mementos are meant to be treasured and admired. So here are plenty of ideas for displaying them.

Feature a special photo in a pillow or shadowbox. Adorn a unique book with tickets or trinkets. You can keep memento displays for yourself or give them as gifts. Gift ideas here include a spa basket, a simple embroidered purse, and jewelry designed with dominos. Creating gifts has never been this much fun!

A Memorable *Vacation*

Use this easy technique to make a pocket-sized accordion book to contain all your travel mementos.

Summer is here and with it come summer vacations! This little booklet is a perfect place to keep track of maps, brochures, receipts, and other travel information to document a favorite trip. You can also use it as a pocket scrapbook to keep postcards and other memorabilia from your vacation. In addition, the blank journal pages inside can be used to jot down notes about what you did on your trip or to display pictures.

You Will Need

- Large sheet of handmade paper (at least 12½ by 23 inches)
- 8 sheets of 8½- by 11-inch paper for the journal pages
- Pencil
- Scissors
- Glue
- Metal ruler or yardstick
- Bone folder
- Three colors of ¼-inch ribbon, each 48 inches long
- Needle (with an eye large enough to hold the ribbon)
- An assortment of beads and charms (with holes large enough to fit over the eye of the needle)

1 Measure and cut a 12½- by 23-inch rectangle out of handmade paper. If paper has a design on just one side, place the design facedown.

Begin measuring and folding the paper. Measure 8½ inches down from the top of the paper and make small marks with a pencil across the length of the paper. (This long 4-inch section will be folded up to form the pocket part of the pages.)

Using the pencil marks as a guide, place a metal ruler across the paper and crease the paper with the bone folder. TIP: Using a yardstick to fold up the paper is easier than using a smaller ruler since you don't have to keep moving your guide.

Metal rulers or metal-edged rulers work best when you are using a bone folder.

Fold the 4-inch section up. Make sure both sides of the section are parallel with the ends, then run the bone folder along the crease to make a clean crisp fold.

2 Fold paper in half with pocket side facing out. Make sure ends and sides are lined up and parallel with each other. Run the bone folder along the center fold to make a clean fold.

a

3 Place center fold to the left. Fold top portion of paper to the left, toward the center fold; extend the end ½ inch over the center fold.

Before using the bone folder to crease the fold, make sure the paper is lined up and parallel on the top and bottom edges. Flip the paper over and place the ruler edge even with the edge of the paper; crease the paper that extends past the center fold with bone folder.

Repeat with the back section. Make sure the edge of the paper extends ½ inch over the center fold and crease it as you did on the first side.

4 The folded paper should now look like a W. With the right side of the paper down and the pocket up, the first fold from the left should be ½ inch over, and the next four folds are 5½ inches apart, leaving a ½-inch section at the right side of the booklet.

To finish the ends of the cover, loosely unfold the paper, leaving only the pocket section folded. On the left side of the booklet, cut the creased ½-inch section off the pocket section, which will make this fold less bulky. Cut a diagonal piece off the corner of the top and bottom of the ½-inch section. Place glue on the inside of the section, fold over pocket, and press down securely. Repeat on the other side.

SPECIAL PROJECT TIPS

• Instead of using handmade paper for the cover, why not use a map of the area you are going to visit? Have fun!

• This travel pocket booklet is perfect for a bride and groom to take on their honeymoon. Add a small pocket camera and film, and you have a great wedding gift! You could also adjust the size of this booklet and make a smaller version without pages to hold postage stamps or grocery coupons. The uses are limitless.

b

5 To sew pages into the booklet cover, stack four sheets of 8½ by 11 paper. Fold the stack in half—to 5½ by 8½.

Take the middle page out of the stack and measure 1 inch in from the top and bottom on the fold. Mark with a pencil. Measure 4¼ inches in and mark again for your center hole. Place the sheet back inside the other sheets, hold them loosely to form a V, and push an awl or needle through each mark, making holes through all the pages.

Place the now punched pages in the first V or valley inside the booklet cover. Holding the sheets in place, push an awl or needle through the three holes in the pages through the cover.

SPECIAL PROJECT TIP

• To fit beads on your ribbon in Step 6, you may want to use use a specialty needle. You can use a collapsible-eye beading needle made of wire, available at your local craft or bead store. You could also use a floss threader, which is a "needle" made of plastic string that has a large eye. You can find these in the dental section of a drugstore.

6 Cut ribbon into 24-inch lengths. Thread all three colors onto a needle. Starting at the outside of the booklet, push the needle through the middle hole and pull the ribbon through, leaving a 6-inch tail. Push the needle through the bottom inside hole to the outside of the booklet. Holding the tail in place, pull the ribbon so it is taut.

At this point, you can add a few decorative beads or knots to your ribbon. You'll need beads with large holes to slip over the bulky ribbon. (You could also use string or embroidery floss to sew in your pages; they will allow you to use a smaller-eyed needle and smaller beads.)

To finish, make a long stitch up through the top hole into the inside and pull the ribbon taut. Go down through the center inside hole to the outside of the booklet. Make sure the ribbon is taut and then tie a knot over the long stitch with the two tails. (If you are using a silky ribbon, add a drop of glue to the knot. This will hold it together.) You can also embellish the tails with beads or knots.

Repeat this process with the other set of pages to fasten them inside the book.

SPECIAL PROJECT TIP

• You can decorate the outside cover of this booklet with postcards or a small map of your destination. You can stamp, use stickers, or use one or more of the many other embellishments that are available on the cover or on the inside pockets.

Altered *Books*

Use an old book to display your favorite mementos.

When it comes to creative projects, few pursuits are as hot as a technique called "altered books." At their simplest, altered books are real books that are used as the base for a new piece of art. Some practitioners stamp, paint, draw, color, and paste new objects over the base of an existing book using tools and tricks often used in scrapbooking. Others use the book to create new three-dimensional art objects celebrating a special memory or other important personal experience.

If you'd like to try your hand at this project, here are two examples that may help inspire your artistic impulses.

A Romantic Keepsake

This book is a collection of items celebrating memorabilia from a grandmother. The edges of the book are tied open with a piece of pink material from the sash of a favorite dress. A handmade doily, a small silver spoon from a honeymoon trip, a favorite piece of jewelry, a pearl necklace, and a few dried flowers enhance the romance.

Oversized books provide the best platform for three-dimensional art collages. These books don't need to be harmed during the process of altering them. In this book, the items were secured with small pins, carefully worked through the top two or three pages on each side. The finished piece can be displayed beautifully on a plate stand on a bureau or dresser.

A Trip of a Lifetime

Here an old ledger serves as the platform for a collection of items that evoke a treasured trip to Paris. The edges of the book are tied open with a luxurious strip of raw silk. Favorite sayings are stamped on a variety of papers and then attached to the book with snippets of ribbon, string, and slips of metallic cord. Old postcards are added, one attached to the book with two tiny clothespins (available at your local craft store). The heart shape, cut from a scrap of card stock and rubber-stamped with an appropriate sentiment, is further enhanced by being cut with decorative scissors to leave a pinked edge on the paper. Small scrapbook metal holders add further dimension to the piece, and a vintage button, still on its Parisian paper card, captures other wonderful memories.

Indoor *Art*

Turn a simple wooden birdhouse into a decorative accent that you can display all year long.

"Outdoor" art can be perfectly at home as elegant indoor art. That's the case with these adorable birdhouses. They started out as simple, unpainted wood pieces purchased for only a couple of dollars at a local hobby store. Using simple techniques, these beauties were created in less than an hour.

1 Using craft paint or spray paint, paint the house in a color of your choice. If you'd like to paint the roof a different color than the body of the house, slip the piece into a plastic bag and simply tape the plastic around the roof line to save time and mess. Add any additional details you'd like with stencils, stamps, or other paint techniques.

SPECIAL PROJECT TIP

• If you'd like to make an even simpler flower from your modeling compound, you can mimic the appearance of a bloom called ranunculus. Roll out a long, very thin piece of the compound and wrap it loosely around the base of a thin artist's brush. Loop the material over and around itself until you're pleased with the result. Slide the flower off the center of the brush, then add a center dot of yellow compound to the middle of the piece. Bake as directed.

2 Print out two color images of your choice, sizing them to fit on either side of your roof. Use a foam brush to apply a liberal coat of decoupage medium to the roof of the house. Center your paper design, and press onto the roof, gently smoothing out any wrinkles or bubbles. Apply a second coat of decoupage medium over the entire roof to seal. Let dry completely, then seal the entire birdhouse with either varnish or a spray sealer.

4 Slide the center of the flower cutout up over the bottom of toothpick and gently twist each petal around the cone-shaped center. Repeat until you like the finished result.

Slip the flower gently off the toothpick and flatten the bottom slightly. Bake as directed by the manufacturer until the flower is set, then adhere it to the birdhouse with a good-quality adhesive.

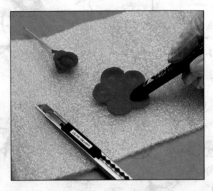

3 Modeling compounds come in a wide variety of colors and can be shaped in a number of ways. Once the design is finished, harden pieces by placing them in a low oven for less than half an hour.

We decided to add rosebuds and leaves to our birdhouses as an accent. A particularly easy way to fashion three-dimensional flowers is by using a plastic "cookie cutter" designed for use in making cake decorations. We found ours in our local craft store.

To make a simple rosebud, form a small cone of modeling compound and place it on the end of a toothpick. Roll out a thin circle of the compound and stamp out one or more simple daisy-type shapes. Using a craft knife, cut between the edges of each petal. Place the flower cutout on a soft surface and then use a pencil eraser to press each petal until it curls and lifts off the surface.

SPECIAL PROJECT TIP

• Special rubberized "push-out" molds allow you to make dozens of leaves, faces, or other shapes in minutes. You can find these at your local craft shop.

A Memory *Pillow*

This clever project features a prized photograph, printed on fabric and then sewn into a throw pillow to keep memories close at hand.

Have a wedding that you'd like to remember? Surprise the bride with a pillow that has a photo of her special day printed on ink jet fabric. Or celebrate an anniversary, birthday, or other special occasion by adding a photo of the event to this adorable pillow.

You Will Need

- One 8½- by 11-inch sheet of paper-backed cotton poplin ink jet fabric
- Computer scanner and print or digital photo
- Ink jet printer
- ½ yard Dupioni silk
- Fray Check
- ¾ yard 100 percent cotton print
- 18 inches square fleece or thin quilt batting
- 18-inch pillow form
- 2⅛ yards tasseled fringe
- Neutral all-purpose thread
- Sewing machine
- Self-healing mat
- Acrylic ruler
- Rotary cutter
- Iron

Getting Started

Select a photo to feature as the center of your pillow. Scan the photo or download it from a digital camera or CD. Adjust the photo as desired. Our sample photo had a very busy background, so we cropped it in a white oval to focus on the wedding cake. Size your photo to fit on your sheet of ink jet compatible fabric. For our sheet of 8½- by 11-inch ink jet fabric, we sized our photo to allow at least ½ inch all around the image for seam allowances. Print your image on a piece of paper to test color balance, resolution, and brightness. Adjust if necessary.

Iron the paper backing of a sheet of ink jet fabric. Insert ink jet fabric in the printer (fabric side down in an up-and-over printer, fabric side up in a straight-through printer) and print. Allow the ink to dry.

Remove the paper backing and rinse, following manufacturer's directions. Dry; trim seam allowances to ½ inch all around the print. Our finished piece measured 8½ by 10 inches. Fit sewing machine with all-purpose sewing thread in bobbin and upper machine. Install the straight/zigzag foot.

NOTE: Dupioni silk ravels easily, so cut it just before you are ready to sew, or seal cut edges with a narrow bead of seam sealant, such as Fray Check.

We used a ½-inch seam allowance throughout this project, unless otherwise noted.

To achieve the look of a full, pudgy pillow, the pillow shell is cut slightly smaller than the 18-inch pillow form, making it full but not packed too tightly.

3 Cut two 5- by 11-inch strips of silk. Stitch one strip to each side of center panel. Press seam allowances toward outside edge. Cut two 4½- by 18½-inch strips of silk. Stitch on top and bottom of center panel. Press seam allowance toward outside edge. Press pillow top well. Pillow top should measure approximately 18 inches square. **TIP:** To avoid dog-eared corners, fold your pillow top in half and then in half again. Cut corners with a rounded edge rather than square.

1 Using a self-healing mat, ruler, and rotary cutter, cut from your silk two 2- by 10-inch strips for the sides of your pillow and two 2- by 8½-inch pieces for the top and bottom.

Fold strips in half lengthwise with wrong sides together; press with a dry iron. Pin one strip along each side of the ink jet print with raw edges even. Stitch. Pin one strip along the top and bottom of the ink jet print with raw edges even. Stitch.

2 From your cotton print fabric, cut four 2- by 10-inch strips. Pin one strip along each side. Stitch. With wrong side facing up, press seam allowances toward outside edges. Turn over and press again, leaving fold of the Dupioni silk strip toward the center panel. Stitch one strip along top and bottom. Stitch and press.

4 Open the pillow top and use as a pattern to cut one piece of fleece and one piece of print fabric for the pillow back. With wrong side of pillow top facing up, position the fleece and pillow top together. Stitch together using ¼-inch seam allowance. Pin fringe around the periphery of the pillow top. Stitch through all layers using ¼-inch seam allowance. Place pillow back over front, right sides facing. Stitch using ½-inch seam allowance, leaving an opening to stuff pillow form.

Turn pillow right side out and stuff. Hand sew opening closed.

A Thistle *Purse*

This technique and pattern produce an elegant thistle design that can embellish any item.

This embroidery pattern uses several different stitching techniques to create an attractive Scottish thistle. We embroidered our pattern on a piece of raw silk that we later used to create a small purse, using a purchased pattern and handle (see Special Project Tip). This technique will work equally well to add this design to tea or bath towels; it can be worked on a purchased tote bag or on clothing, or enlarged to use on a decorative pillow top.

Getting Started

• Place fabric on stretcher bars using thumbtacks. Space tacks 1½ to 2 inches apart. Place your tacks in the outer area so the holes will not show on finished work. Stretcher bars (available in needlework shops) will eliminate fabric circles left from using a hoop

• If using a hoop, wrap it with strips of fabric.

• Use 12- to 14-inch thread lengths.

• To begin stitching, place a small knot in the end of the thread. To end threads, slip the needle/thread under two stitches on the back side. Slide the needle/thread between fabrics, going 1 inch away from stitching, come up with needle/thread, and clip thread close to fabric. Cover basted outline with embroidery stitches. When stitching is completed, remove any basting thread that is showing.

• Design can be worked using other embroidery stitches: use the stem stitch for flower stem or the satin stitch for the flower base, for example.

Basic Stitches

Long Stitch with Couching

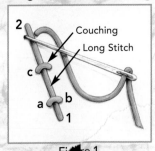

Figure 1

How to work the
_____ with

_____ ch, bring the
_____ going down
_____ all six
_____ lie flat.
_____ stitch over
_____ Using the
_____ loss, bring
_____ (a) taking
_____ at (b), come
_____ tinue along
_____ long stitch.

Pattern is shown actual size

You Will Need

• 5- by 6-inch piece of ivory batiste (sheer) fabric
• Raw silk (or other fabric)
• Embroidery floss in dark forest green, medium forest green, and light yellow green
• Hand-dyed cotton thread in both light and dark dusty rose
• Waterproof black marker
• Green sewing thread to match medium forest green
• Black and white sewing thread
• 8- by 8-inch stretcher bars OR embroidery hoop
• Thumbtacks (for stretcher bars)
• General sewing supplies (pins, ruler, pinking shears, scissors, embroidery needle, sewing machine)
• Masking tape

SPECIAL PROJECT TIP

• **Evening Purse:** A pattern and instructions for making this small purse are available from BagLady Press, (888)222-4523, or visit www.baglady.com. BagLady Press also offers handbag handles and chains to complete the purse.

The handle we chose was No. ML52g gold, coupled with a 13-inch gold-plated bag chain, No. C2G.

If you create this design using the purse kit, trace the pattern front onto the batiste fabric and center the design within the pattern.

Stem Stitch

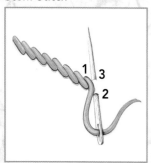

Figure 2

Chain Stitch

Figure 3

Straight Stitch

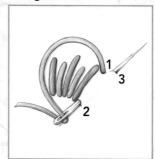

Figure 4

Satin Stitch

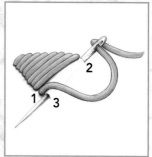

Figure 5A

How to Work the Stem Stitch:

Keep the thread on the lower side of the needle while stitching along the drawn line. Bring the needle up at 1, go down at 2, bring the needle up at 3 halfway between 1 and 2. Repeat 1-3; continue in this manner until area is completed.

How to Work the Chain Stitch:

Bring the needle up at 1; let the thread lie on top of the fabric forming a loop. Holding the loop in place, go down at 2 next (no space between) to 1, up at 3 crossing over the thread to begin the next chain stitch.

How to Work the Straight Stitch:

Bring the needle up at 1 and go down at 2, being sure the threads lie flat and you have not pulled the stitch too tightly.

Repeat this until all the straight stitches are in place. For the petals, use random lengths.

How to Work the Satin Stitch:

Bring the needle up at 1; go across the area on a slant going down at 2 (center basting line). Bring the needle up at 3; repeat 1-2, working down one side of leaf. End thread at the base of leaf. Go back up to tip of leaf and work other side.

Leaf Stitch Guide

Figure 5B

1 Select your fabric. (We used an 8- by 8-inch piece fabric, and pink around batiste fabric. Center the place. Trace the design on the fabric using a water center design on the silk, and pin in place. Using batiste to silk. If using stretcher bars, attach fab baste around the traced design, using green se a clear outline of the flowers, stem, and leave Do not baste the long petals of the flowers s

ow to Wo Long Stitc Couching:

For the long stit needle up at 1, g at 2, being sure strands of thread Place a couching the long stitch. U single strand of f the needle up at the needle down up at (c), and con the length of the

2 Starting at the bottom of the basted stem, place the long stitch. Use six strands (do not separate) of dark forest green embroidery floss. Do not end the thread after the long stitch is placed. You will need to adjust the length of the thread as the couching is worked. When the long stitch is in place, slide the needle/thread into the upper right corner on the wrong side, away from the stitching area. Leave the thread slightly loose across the basted stem line. Be careful to keep this thread out of working area. Couching is worked like a spaced overcast stitch. Couch over the long stitch using one strand of dark forest green. Do not pull the long stitch or couching stitch too tight.

3 Starting on the left side, stitch along the top basted edge of the flower base. Use the stem stitch with two strands of medium forest green floss. Start on the left side of the flower base and place vertical rows of the chain stitch using two strands of medium forest green floss. To begin the stitching, slip the needle/thread under the stem stitch, working the chain stitch down along the outside edge of the flower base. When a row is complete, run your thread between fabrics, up to the stem stitch. Work the rows of chain stitches close to the previous row. TIP: If black fabric shows at the top between the stem and chain stitches, fill in with a row of the stem stitch. Start on the left side next to the top edge of stem stitch, working out, placing the flower petals using the straight stitch. Use the two shades of dusty rose floss, starting with the dark. Place random lengths of straight stitches across the area, leaving a space between the stitches. Fill in the spaces using the light dusty rose.

4 Starting on the left side of the large leaf at the first jagged point, work from the center baste line outward. Stitch the outer portion of the leaf using the satin stitch and two strands of medium forest green floss. Follow the arrows on the leaf stitch guide (figure 5B on page 82). As you work down the leaf, it will be necessary to angle a stitch slightly to keep in line with the center; this will leave a space between stitches. To cover the black fabric showing, fill in with a short satin stitch.

If you have not worked this type of stitch before, it might be helpful to continue the single basting line to the bottom tip of the leaf. NOTE: In the leaf area, the center area could end up being larger or smaller than the basted line. This area can be filled in when the center is completed. Start at the top of center area to complete the leaf. Use the satin stitch and two strands of light yellow green floss.

Wedding *Season*

These handmade invitations for a shower—and a wedding—can make a special day even better.

Spring and early summer are popular times for brides and grooms to walk down the aisle. Add to that the parties and showers that are part of the events, and you have a perfect opportunity to show off your creativity with a special invitation to a special day.

An invitation is the first impression guests will have of a party. Handcrafted invitations convey the theme of your event and your style and personality. They also make your guests feel extra special!

By using paper crafting techniques, rubber stamps, and a few extra items, you can make the invitation feel as nice as the event itself.

A CHECKLIST FOR INVITATIONS

Want to make your own personal invitations? Start with a few questions:

When is the event?
Allow enough time realistically to complete the invitations, address them, and get them in the mail in a timely fashion. For weddings, mail invitations six to eight weeks ahead of the date. For other invites, two weeks is generally enough lead-time.

How many people will be invited?
Know how many invitations you will be making. Wedding invitations may number in the hundreds but you may need fewer than a dozen for a child's party. Consider the complexity of the design you've chosen in light of the number of invites you'll need to make.

What do I want the invitations to look like?
Do you have a theme or a certain color in mind? Should the invitations be contemporary or traditional? The style is up to you, but keep your envelope in mind as you plan your invitation. Traditional invitation envelopes are about 5½ by 7½ inches, but beautiful invitations can be created to fit business size (#10), greeting card (A-2, A-6) and homemade envelopes, among others. NOTE: A full sheet of 8½- by 11-inch paper will make two folded, or four postcard-style, invitations when cut. These will fit into an A-2 sized envelope. You can find envelopes at stationery, business supply, stamp stores, or invitation companies (their large, bound books can be found at wedding shops, office and paper supply stores).

What is my budget?
Paper can be expensive, so keep your design in mind as you browse for paper choices. Remember, postage will add to your total. Bulky, square, and oversized invitations cost more than the standard postage rate. Take a completed invitation to the post office and ask them to weigh it for you before you make all of them.

You Will Need

- 5½- by 8½-inch card stock (white and colored)
- Rubber stamp
- Pigment ink in desired color (we used black)
- Embossing powder in desired color (we used clear)
- Watercolor paints or dye ink pads
- Paintbrush
- Water
- Glitter glue (we used Stickles Opalescent White)
- Craft knife and cutting mat
- Ruler
- Bone folder
- Heat-embossing tool

1 Fold card stock in half and crease well with bone folder. Open the card and stamp the image inside the front cover with pigment ink. Immediately sprinkle the image with embossing powder and shake the excess powder back into the jar. (The embossing will help contain the paint in the area you are working in the next step.) Heat the powder with the heat tool until the powder just melts. (TIP: Be sure that your embossing powder jar is closed, so that you don't blow the powder over your work space. Do not overheat the powder as it can bubble or scorch the paper.) Allow image to cool for a moment.

2 Wet your paintbrush and pick up some of the paint or ink. If you are using ink pads as your paint source, squeeze the closed ink pad's cover into the pad itself. When you open the pad, there will be a smudge of ink on the cover. Simply dip your wet brush into this smudge and apply to your image, shading as desired.

3 Find the center of the stamped page with your ruler. Without scoring through the image, draw the tip of your bone folder along the edge of a ruler on that center line to score the paper from top to bottom, above and below the image. Use a cutting mat and a sharp craft knife to trim around the image on the right side only. Do not cut past the scored center line. (This will allow the image to pop out.) Carefully free the cut edge to make sure you have cut completely through the paper.

With the invitation oriented like a book, fold the front cover back on itself so that the edge lines up with the fold. The embossed image should pop free on the right side.

4 Stamp the invitation wording on the inside of your card. Stamp the inside of the invitation on the far left side of the card, so that your text doesn't show when you close the invitation.

You can now mount the folded card to a slightly larger piece of coordinating card stock for emphasis.

5 Open the bottle of glitter glue and give a gentle squeeze to expel any air that might be trapped in the nozzle. Apply glitter to the stamped image wherever you feel it will enhance the design. Allow this to dry completely before handling. TIP: You can save this step for the very end of the assembly process. Apply the glitter and let the invitations dry for several hours before you fill in the party information and mail.

A Simple, Elegant Wedding Invitation

You can make a beautiful, traditional wedding invitation to match the bride's colors by using two 5½- by 7½-inch sheets of card stock—one in a dark shade and the second in a lighter shade. Pick an appropriate rubber stamp that matches your theme and some beautiful silky ribbon in a color that matches your invitation. You'll also need a sheet of translucent vellum, which you can run through your computer printer to fill in the dates and details of the wedding.

Print your text on the vellum and trim it to 5 by 7 inches. (Allow an extra inch or so on the top margin of the invitation before the text begins, to accommodate the ribbon.) It's easier to align your text if you print on a full-sized sheet of vellum and then cut it.

Rubber stamp your chosen image on the light-colored card stock. Play with this step a bit to be sure that you are pleased with the placement of the stamped image. Let the ink on this sheet dry.

Place the light-colored card stock facedown on a clean, flat surface. Lightly spray the back side of the card stock with spray adhesive, then adhere this piece to your larger piece of card stock.

To finish the invitation with ribbon, center the printed and trimmed vellum on the assembled card stock. Punch two holes about ½ inch apart centered in the margin at the top of the vellum sheet.

Be sure to go through all three layers. Feed both ends of ribbon to the back side, cross them, and feed them to the front again through the opposite holes. Pull snug, but don't rip the holes. Trim ribbon to desired length.

SPECIAL PROJECT TIP

• A traditional text for a wedding invitation might read something like this:

Mr. and Mrs. Stephen John McCall

request the honor of your presence

at the marriage of their daughter

Colleen Marie

to

Mr. Jason Allen Williams

on Saturday, the fourteenth of August

Two thousand and four

At four o'clock in the afternoon

St. Mary's Basilica

Minneapolis, Minnesota

If you are using protective tissue sheets, place them over the printed wording on your invitation. The reply card is always placed next to the invitation, with any other enclosures (separate reception information, maps, etc.) in front of the reply card. Insert all enclosures with printed side up. Place the assembled invitation and enclosures into the inner, unsealed envelope so that the printed wording or cover design is facing up and you can read it. Slide this inner envelope into the outer envelope with guests' names facing you. If you are not using an inner envelope, you also place the invitation in the outer envelope facing up.

SPECIAL PROJECT TIP

• When you use spray adhesives, it's a big help to make a spray box to contain the small beads of glue that can become airborne. It can be a large paper box or carton with high sides. Cover the bottom of the box with clean copy paper so that you don't pick up flecks from the inside of the box. Don't use newsprint, as the ink will transfer to your invitation. You will need to replace the liner from time to time, or simply add another layer on top of the first.

Fun and Funky
Photo Albums

Turn an inexpensive pocket photo album into a personalized portfolio—or a great gift.

Although scrapbooking has become a wildly popular craft project in recent years, it's a good bet that many of us still have photos scattered throughout our homes. Or perhaps you've always planned to create an entire scrapbook celebrating your vacations through the years—but you just haven't quite gotten to it yet.

This project lets you enjoy the outward appearance of a personalized scrapbook without the time investment: Simply "repackage" an inexpensive photo album from your local discount store into a personalized portfolio.

Photo pocket albums are available in different sizes and can hold up to 400 photos. The easiest albums to work with for this project have binder-type clasps inside to hold the pages.

These little items also make great gifts. Consider making a wedding album, baby picture album, or a vacation album for a friend.

Finally, one of the fun things about re-covering albums is that there is such a wide variety of specialty papers from which to choose. Consider using wrapping paper, old maps, handmade specialty paper, scrapbook paper, or even specialty bookbinder's cloth. The only requirement is that the material you choose be opaque enough so that you won't see the pattern on the original cover through the paper.

SPECIAL PROJECT TIP

• You can further personalize a premade photo album by using one of the hundreds of scrapbooking embellishments available. You can find metal pieces, tags, labels, and even stickers. They add a special touch to any album.

Getting Started

It's a good idea to review all of the steps for this project before you begin.

To cut the outside cover paper to size, lay the album open on a table. Measure the length of the album and add 2 inches. NOTE: This project looks best if the top and bottom of your paper reaches around the edges and all the way to the clasp. Therefore, to determine the height, measure how far it is from either the bottom or the top of the album to the outer edge of the binder clasp. Double this number, and add it to the measured height. (For instance, if it is 1 inch from the top of the album to the outer edge of the binder clasp, add 2 inches to the measured height of the book.)

Cut the piece of paper for the outside cover to the above measurements.

You Will Need

- Pocket photo album (binder style)
- Ruler
- Scissors
- Pencil
- Decorative or specialty paper for cover
- Paper plate
- White craft glue
- Washcloth
- Small foam paint roller
- Brush

Optional:
- Embellishments or ribbon

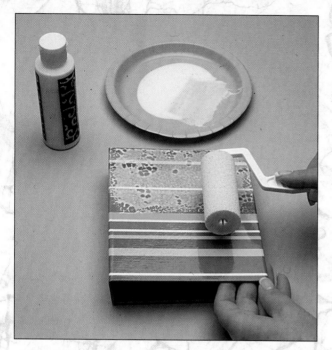

1 Place the cut paper right side down under the open album. Make sure the album is lying flat, and center the paper under the album. Mark the corners lightly with a pencil for easier placement of the paper when gluing. (If you are using a patterned paper that has an obvious horizontal or vertical line, you will need to be very careful in your placement of your paper when you are gluing.)

Put a 3-inch circle of white craft glue on a paper plate. (If you can locate it, a specialty adhesive called bookbinder's glue is designed specially for applications such as this, but it's not crucial.) Keep your hands free of glue. Keep a washcloth close to the working area so you can clean them if necessary. If you get glue on the right side of your paper, it will leave a mark.

Place clean scrap paper on your work area. (Shiny newspaper sales ads work well because the finish will help keep your paper from being accidentally glued to the work surface. Don't use newspaper because the ink can smear on your project.)

Roll a foam roller in the glue, then roll it onto the front section of the outside of the album cover. Make sure there is an even coating of glue all the way to the edges. Quickly place the album cover onto your cut paper so it lines up with the marks you made. Once the cover is placed, you may not be able to move it, so be careful. Before applying any pressure or smoothing the paper, turn the album over and make sure the paper is lying flat, with no bubbles or creases. Now smooth the paper gently with your hands all the way to the edges.

Next, glue the spine with the roller on the outside of the album. Make sure to go all the way to the edges with your glue. Carefully fold the paper over the spine, smoothing it down with your hands. If there are any crevices or folds on the spine, make sure the paper is glued down into those areas. (That extra paper allows the album to open and close without ripping the paper.)

Glue the back side of the outside of the album next. Smooth the paper into place. At this point, the paper should be glued over the entire front surface of the album with about a 1-inch overlap around the edges.

2 With the album open and the covered side down, trim off the corners, leaving a width of paper that is a little larger than the thickness of the album cover. Snipping the corners of your paper will keep your corner folds from being too bulky.

Fold the left overlapping portion of paper over the side edge of the album. Make a clean crease against the edge of the album. Pull the paper back and apply glue to the flap with a brush. Make sure the glue goes all the way to the edge of the paper. Once the glue is applied, fold the paper snugly around the edge of the album and smooth it down. Repeat on the opposite side of the album. Now fold over the top and bottom flaps of paper following the same process. Let dry.

SPECIAL PROJECT TIP

• Another fun way to use this type of covered album is to insert recipes written on index cards instead of photos. Smaller albums work great for this. You can use the recipe album as a shower gift for a bride-to-be or as a gift for your children. Or you can make one for yourself that has all of your favorite recipes in it, and you won't have to go looking for the cookbook anymore!

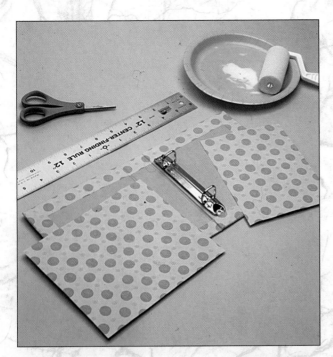

• You can finish the front of your album a variety of ways. Here we glued a simple brass nameplate (purchased at our local office supply store) to our cover with Tacky Glue. We then stamped a phrase on card stock and slipped it inside.

3 To cut the paper for the inside of the cover, lay the album open and measure the left side of the album between the outside edge and the metal clasp; subtract ¼ inch. Measure the height of the left side cover and subtract ½ inch. Cut a piece of paper to this size. Mark a small "L" in one of the corners to help you remember which side this cut piece matches.

Repeat for the right side piece.

Before gluing your papers, lay them in place and check to make sure the tops and bottoms are ¼ inch from the edge. The sides of the papers facing the clasp should extend all the way to the clasp.

Glue in place, one side at a time. NOTE: When you're applying the glue for these pieces, run the roller from the center of the paper to the edge. If you roll from edge to edge, you may accidentally flip your paper over and get glue on the right side of the piece, which will leave a mark.

Allow to dry.

SPECIAL PROJECT TIP

• If you like, you can add a piece of ribbon to this book to tie it closed. In Step 3, before gluing the inside portions of paper to the cover, cut two pieces of ribbon, each about 10 inches long. Brush glue on the bottom 4 inches of each piece of ribbon, and place crosswise on either side of the inside of the cover. Let dry before proceeding with Step 3.

A Personal *Shadow Box*

Turn your favorite photos into a unique piece of art by transferring them onto marble.

This project makes use of a prepackaged kit that lets users transfer photos onto a marble coaster. The kit, available from a company called Tilano Fresco, contains four marble coasters, specialty paper, and other products that will lift an image from any photo and adhere it to the enclosed marble. (See Special Project Tip for ordering information.)

While the coasters themselves are decorative, we wanted to use this product in a unique way to create a piece of art, so we mounted our finished project in an inexpensive shadow box.

You Will Need

- Several personal snapshots
- One Decorative Marble Coaster Kit
- One 11- by 14-inch shadow box, at least 1 inch deep
- Access to a professional copier store, such as Kinko's
- Double-sided Velcro

1 Pick four good-quality snapshots that have a common theme. (We used four images from a favorite trip to New Orleans.) Consider family photos, pictures of your pets, photos from your garden, or anything else that appeals to you.

The tiles used here measure 4 inches square. Cut a piece of paper to that size and lay it over your images, making sure that the section of the photo you wish to transfer will fit nicely on the tile. (You can photocopy the images at a larger or smaller percentage to get more of the picture on the tiles.)

Once you're satisfied, take your images to a local copier store and photocopy them onto the specialty transfer paper. Complete instructions are included with the tile coaster kit. Images can be transferred in color, in black and white, or, as we did in our example, by photocopying our images using the "sepia" feature on a commercial photocopier. (Ask for assistance at the store if you need it to select this feature.)

2 If you wish, you can add an antiqued patina to the tile coaster. Place a few drops of the antiquing glaze on the tile and work it into the surface, following manufacturer's instructions.

SPECIAL PROJECT TIP

- The Tilano Fresco coaster kit we used can be ordered from Tilano Decorative Products, (866)877-4031 or visit www.tilanofresco.com. The kit contains four marble coasters, three sheets of specialty transfer paper, antiquing and sealing glazes, sandpaper, a brush, and a tack cloth.

3 Cut the specialty photocopier paper to size, place it on the tile, and then wet the back of the paper to transfer your design.

Once our tiles had dried, we mounted them using double-sided Velcro in our shadow box. You can now display your personalized art either on a wall or as a decorative item on a table or bureau.

Autumn *Chill-Chaser*

This gorgeous crocheted hat and scarf make use of the fun new eyelash yarn that's so popular right now.

94

The color plum is so hot in fashion this fall the trendsetters are calling it the new black. Combine it with the hottest trend in yarn, eyelash, and you have a hat and scarf set that really sizzles.

This hat, made from the directions below, will fit most adults. (Its circumference is about 20 to 21 inches.) The scarf is about 4½ by 56 inches.

If you prefer a different color, we suggest you select a variegated eyelash yarn first. Then pick a solid color yarn to match any of the colors in the variegated. Your set will look equally great!

You Will Need

- 1 oz./50 yards 80 percent acrylic/20 percent nylon worsted weight yarn
- 3.5 oz./180 yards 100 percent polyester eyelash yarn
- K (6.5 mm) crochet hook or size required to obtain gauge
- Split ring marker
- Ruler or tape measure (to check gauge)
- Scissors
- Yarn needle

SPECIAL PROJECT TIP

- If you would like to make a smaller hat for a teen or a child (about 19 inches in circumference), stop increasing at the end of Round 10, working even on 60 stitches for the remaining rounds. If you would like a wider scarf, simply make a longer chain to begin. If you would like a longer scarf, work more rows. Remember to buy extra eyelash yarn if you are making a larger scarf.

Basic Stitches

Crochet Stitches used in this project

Chain (ch)

Half double crochet (hdc)

Double crochet (dc)

Slip stitch (sl st)

Round (rnd)

Repeat (rep)

Chain Stitch

Half Double Crochet

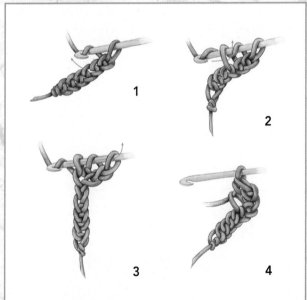

Double Crochet

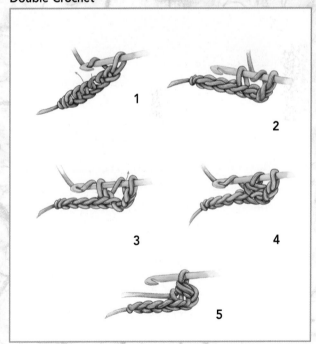

Slip Stitch

Hat

GAUGE: At the end of Round 5, the piece should measure 4 inches in diameter.

PATTERN NOTES:
Items included within ( ) are informational.

Items included within [ ] indicate an action that will be repeated the specified number of times.

Leave 6-inch tails when beginning and ending yarn.

Move marker to first stitch of each round.

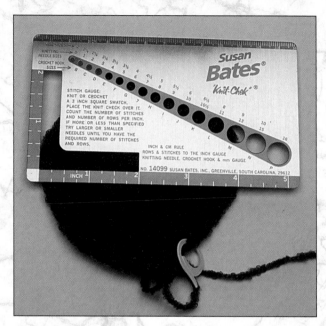

Rnd 1: Starting at top of hat with solid color yarn, ch 2; 6 hdc in 2nd ch from hook. (6 sts, mark first st made)

Rnd 2: Work 2 hdc in each st around. (12 sts)

Rnd 3: *Hdc in next st; 2 hdc in next st; rep from * around. (18 sts)

Rnd 4: *[Hdc in next st] two times; 2 hdc in next st; rep from * around. (24 sts)

Rnd 5: *[Hdc in next st] three times; 2 hdc in next st; rep from * around. (30 sts) TIP: If your circle is smaller than gauge (above), switch to a larger hook; if your circle is larger, switch to a smaller hook and work again.

Rnd 6: *[Hdc in next st] four times; 2 hdc in next st; rep from * around. (36 sts)

Rnd 7: *[Hdc in next st] five times; 2 hdc in next st; rep from * around. (42 sts)

Rnd 8: *[Hdc in next st] six times; 2 hdc in next st; rep from * around. (48 sts)

Rnd 9: *[Hdc in next st] seven times; 2 hdc in next st; rep from * around. (54 sts)

Rnd 10: *[Hdc in next st] eight times; 2 hdc in next st; rep from * around. (60 sts)

Rnd 11: *[Hdc in next st] nine times; 2 hdc in next st; rep from * around. (66 sts)

Rnd 12: Hdc in each st around. (66 sts)

Rnds 13–16: Rep Rnd 12.

Rnd 17: Rep Rnd 12, working off last 3 loops of final hdc with eyelash yarn; drop plum to wrong side and cut leaving a 6-inch tail. (66 sts)

Rnd 18: With eyelash yarn, rep Rnd 12.

Rnd 19: Rep Rnd 18.

Rnd 20: Rep Rnd 18, ending with sl st in first st of rnd. Fasten off.

FINISHING: With yarn needle, weave in yarn ends.

Scarf

GAUGE: 10 sts; 6 rows = 3 inches

ADDITIONAL PATTERN NOTE: Ch 3 at beginning of row counts as first dc.

Row 1: With eyelash yarn, ch 17; dc in 4th ch from hook; *dc in next ch; rep from * across. (15 sts – first 3 chs skipped count as 1 st)

Row 2: Turn, ch 3; dc in each st across. (15 sts). Repeat row 2 until scarf measures desired length or you run out of yarn. Fasten off and weave in yarn ends.

SPECIAL PROJECT TIP

• If you are having difficulty finding the top two loops of the stitch to work into, you can work your double crochet between the stitches of the previous row. This will change your gauge. Your scarf will be about ¼ inch wider and about ½ inch shorter per each 7 rows worked.

A Spa Gift Basket

This luxurious spa basket, complete with an easy-to-make hand mitt, makes an inexpensive but personal gift for a friend.

Few luxuries are as heartwarming as a long soak in a warm bath. If you know someone who's feeling a little down in the dumps these days, why not pamper her with a personal spa basket? The gift doesn't have to be expensive. Simply find an attractive basket and tuck in a few sweet-scented oils, a candle or two, and perhaps some bubble bath, just for fun.

To make this gift truly personal, you can also include a handmade bath mitt, perfect for scrubbing in the tub. Best of all, this handy little mitt can be made in about 15 minutes from two washcloths—a gift both pleasant and unexpected.

You Will Need

- Two washcloths
- Paper
- Pencil
- ½-inch elastic
- Ribbon
- Scissors, pins, and sewing machine

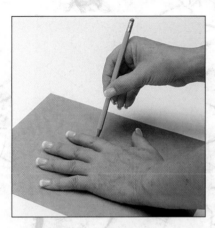

1 Place your hand on a piece of paper and spread your fingers out as widely as possible. Lightly trace the outline of your hand with a pencil. Remove your hand. Pencil in a second darker line about 1 inch outside your previous outline. (You want to leave extra room for your sewing allowances and to make sure that the glove fits nicely.) NOTE: If you are making this as a present for someone who has larger hands than you do, you may want to make your allowance even larger.

Cut out the pattern on the second line, and square off the bottom.

2 Place your paper pattern on one washcloth, lining up the bottom edge of the glove with a finished edge of the washcloth.

Cut the pattern. Repeat with the other washcloth. TIP: We found it easier to cut the washcloths individually rather than try to cut both at the same time.

To prevent the cut edges of your washcloths from raveling, it may be necessary to zigzag stitch around the cut edges with matching thread.

Special Project Tip

- Washcloths with a banded edge work beautifully and add a nice detail to this mitt.

3 Cut two pieces of elastic 1½ inches shorter than the width at the opening of the glove. Sew the elastic in place about 1½ inches up from the bottom edge of both mitt pattern pieces.

4 Cut a piece of ribbon about 5 inches long. Fold ribbon in half, creating a loop. Place ribbon even with outside edge and machine stitch in place. With right sides together, pin front of glove to back and sew using ½-inch seam allowance.

Turn glove right side out.

A Frosty *Pillow*

Use stencils and beads to create a sparkling celebration of the season.

As winter approaches, we're starting to think about the beautiful snowflakes that come with the cold weather. Get a start on the season with this decorative snowflake pillow. (This is a great gift for either yourself or a friend.)

Getting Started

Carefully read all instructions before starting. Choose a stencil image you like or use the snowflake one shown here. These stencils were randomly placed over the area. There is no right or wrong position.

1 Press fabric if necessary. Cut two pieces of Sateen fabric 14½ inches square. Set one aside for pillow back.

Slightly overlap four sheets of white paper on a flat dry surface. Tape the sheets together using painter's tape. Place the piece of fabric on the paper.

Using painter's tape and small pieces of white paper, cover stencil areas that will not be used. (Cover both sides of stencil to cover tape in open areas.) Refer to photograph to see snowflake stencils used.

2 Use ½-inch spouncer for smaller snowflake stencils. Use 1½-inch spouncer for larger snowflakes. Use one plate as a paint palette and the other to tap extra paint off spouncer. Place a small amount of each paint color on one plate, keeping colors separate.

Using prepared stencil, apply paint with a different spouncer for each color. Start with gold paint and the largest stencil. Gently tap fabric with spouncer; cover entire area. Carefully lift stencil to move it to another random area to stencil next snowflake. Stencil medium snowflake in the same manner. Using silver paint, stencil small snowflakes to fill in some of the blank area. Complete the stenciling with the small gold snowflakes. Clean the stencil and spouncer with warm soapy water. Allow fabric to dry for 24 hours.

Place an old piece of sheeting or pillowcase on ironing board. Lay stenciled front side down; iron with a dry iron to heat-set the paint.

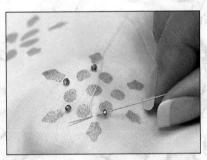

3 Using blue beads and white sewing thread, attach beads as indicated in photograph. For large gold snowflake, sew a bead at the snowflake's very outer tip and another slightly above the square end of the same section. For medium silver snowflake, sew bead between outer circles just above the start of the outer section. Sew through each bead twice as indicated in the illustration below.

You Will Need

- ½ yard white cotton Sateen (we used a fabric called Ultra Sateen by Robert Kaufman)
- ½ yard cotton lining fabric
- Small fabric scrap
- Snowflake stencil with varying sizes (we used No. 28332 "Snowflakes", a Simply Christmas Stencil by Plaid)
- ½-inch and 1½-inch stencil spouncers
- ½ inch painter's tape
- 6 sheets of 8½ by 11 inch white paper
- Fabric paint in gold and silver (we used Pebeo's Setacolor Opaque fabric paints, No. 45 Shimmer Gold and No. 60 Shimmer Silver)
- Paper plates
- Small blue beads (we used Westrim Crafts Blue Rochaille Beads No. 140-VE-021, size 10/1/2, style 140)
- White sewing thread
- 14 inch square pillow insert
- 1½ yards white cord

4 TO FINISH THE PILLOW: Cut two pieces of lining fabric 14½ inches square. Using a ½-inch seam allowance, baste one piece of the lining (right side) to the back side of the stenciled front and one to the back side of the back piece.

Pin the flat fabric edge of the cord to the outer edge of the right side of the pillow front; overlap the ends of the cord on the bottom edge of the fabric. Trim as needed and stitch in place.

With right sides of the Sateen fabric together, stitch around the fabric, leaving an opening on the bottom to insert pillow. Insert pillow and slipstitch opening closed.

SPECIAL PROJECT TIP

• To sew on the beads, bring the needle and thread up to the front side of the fabric, place a bead on the needle and take the needle back down into the fabric. Come back up and sew through the bead a second time going down into the fabric. Continue in this manner until all the beads are placed.

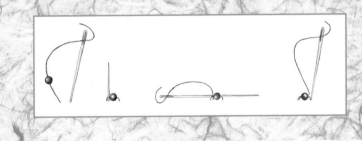

Your Own Domino Jewelry

With rubber stamps, a few domino tiles, and some creativity, you can make a boxful of wonderful, unique jewelry.

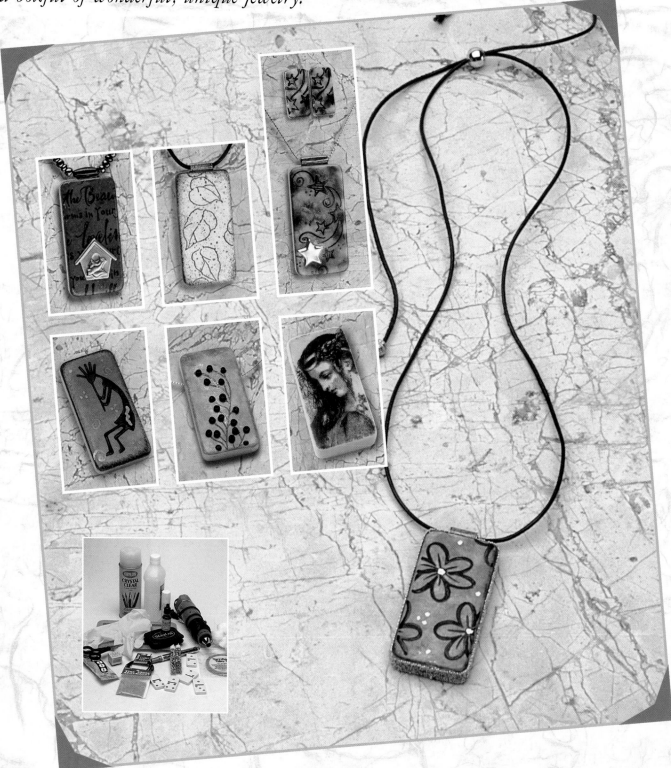

These little beauties are a quick accessory, or the perfect gift. Better yet, they're so easy to make that you can have a different one for every day of the month! We created several pieces of jewelry, using the techniques shown in the following steps.

SPECIAL PROJECT TIPS

You can vary this project in several ways:

• Attach a pin back to make a brooch instead of a necklace.

• Use smaller dominos or even Scrabble tiles to make earrings.

• Use a drill press with a ⅛-inch glass drill bit to make decorative holes in your domino tiles.

• Drill two or three holes through the width of your domino to make a two or three-strand beaded bracelet.

You Will Need

- Domino tiles
- Disposable gloves
- Solvent ink refills (we used StazOn)
- Permanent black ink pad (we used StazOn)
- Gold or silver leafing pens
- Heat tool
- Rubbing alcohol
- Cotton balls
- Stamp image of your choice
- Strong, clear adhesive (we used E6000) and toothpick for application
- Krylon clear spray sealant
- ¼-inch Terrifically Tacky Tape

- Tiny glass balls (ours were manufactured by Halcraft)
- Leather or satin cording or beading wire
- Miscellaneous beads, charms, and findings (Note: Be sure that you have at least one flat-sided bead that you can attach to the edge or back side of your domino for threading your pendant onto the cording. This bead should have a hole large enough to accommodate your cording or ribbon.)
- Stamp cleaner and scrub pad for cleanup

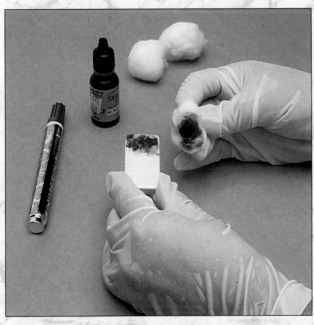

1 CREATING A MARBLED DOMINO BACKGROUND: Cover workspace with paper and put on disposable gloves. (Solvent ink stains hands and nails quickly.)

Moisten cotton ball in alcohol, but do not soak. Drop one or two drops of StazOn refill ink onto cotton ball and dab on smooth side of domino. The alcohol will allow you to blend the color as you work it into the domino, creating a dappled look. Try mixing two different colors for a more dramatic, marbled effect. (If you are using a chalk ink pad, swab the ink pad directly onto the domino to achieve your desired look.) You can leave the ink bright and bold or simply "kiss" the ink pad to the domino for a more subtle edge of color.)

TIP: If the ink won't adhere to your domino, you may need to soak the tile in bleach overnight. This will dissolve the glaze coating on the domino and prepare it for the ink.

2 ADDING A METALLIC GLINT TO YOUR MARBLED DOMINO: Moisten a clean cotton ball with alcohol and dab a metallic leafing pen once onto the ball to transfer a bit of the paint. Work the metallic paint onto the surface of the domino as desired. The colors will bleed together as the alcohol dries. Apply more of the colored solvent ink if it becomes too muted.

When the desired look is achieved, heat-set the ink on the domino with a heat tool.

NOTE: The domino will heat up very quickly, and holds the heat for some time. Be careful not to burn your fingers!

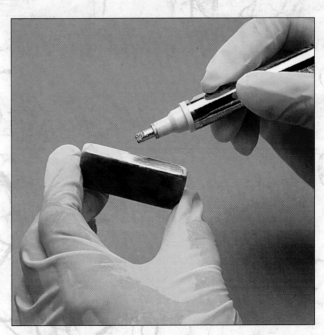

3 EDGING YOUR DOMINO WITH COLOR: Using a leafing pen, color the edge of your domino with a coordinating metallic color. If you prefer to use a chalk ink pad for contrast, simply brush the ink pad along the edge of your domino until you reach the desired effect.

• Always heat-set your inks when making domino jewelry before moving on to the next step.

• Until you heat-set the inks on your domino, you can erase most mistakes with an alcohol-moistened swab.

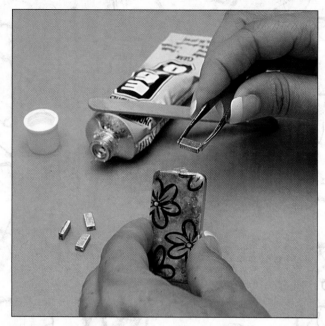

4 ADDING A STAMPED DESIGN: Ink your stamp well with the StazOn ink pad. NOTE: You only need to ink the area you intend to use on the domino. If you are using a large stamp, place it on its back and press the smooth, marbled side of the domino onto the inked surface of the stamp. Apply even pressure, but be careful not to slide the domino or your image will smudge. When using a smaller stamped image, it may be easier to press the stamp directly onto the smooth surface of the domino.

HINT: If your colors don't turn out as expected or your stamped image smudges, moisten a clean cotton ball with alcohol and rub the surface of the domino clean. Most of the ink will come off, and you can reapply your marbled colors to cover what ink remains.

Once you're satisfied, heat-set your stamped image to make it permanent. To finish, spray the domino with a clear sealant to ensure that your image stays put.

5 COMPLETING YOUR PENDANT: We added a few dots of the metallic leafing pen for a subtle touch. Attach a flat-sided bead to the upper edge of the domino, using E6000 glue and a craft stick or toothpick. You may also choose to attach the bead to the back of the domino, in order to keep the edges smooth. If you do so, be sure that the bead is mounted close to the top, or your pendant will flop forward.

6 For this particular pendant, we wrapped ¼-inch Terrifically Tacky Tape around the edges of the domino. Rub your finger firmly along the tape to secure it and remove the red backing. Press the sticky edges into a bowl of tiny glass balls.

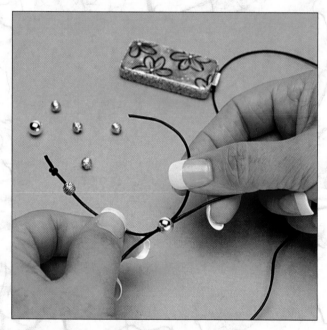

7 THREADING YOUR PENDANT ONTO THE CORDING: Thread the cording through the bead mounted on the domino. There are many ways of securing the cording. If you want to use beads to secure the cording, thread both ends of the cording through one bead, in opposite directions. Attach another bead to each of the free ends of the cording after they have passed through the central bead. Tie a knot at the very end of the cording and snug the beads together by pulling gently on the cording.

Navy Blue and Gold Star Pendant and Earrings

We marbled the domino with blue ink and a gold leafing pen and then heat-set the inks. (See Step 1.) We stamped our image and heat-set it. We cut the prongs off a star-shaped brad and glued the star over one of the stamped stars on the pendant. We accented the edges of the domino with the gold leafing pen. We also used the gold leafing pen to fill in some of the stamped stars on both the pendant and earrings.

Birdhouse Pendant

We colored this tile directly from a chalk ink pad and then we heat-set it. We inked a portion of a large word stamp, set the stamp on its back, and pressed the domino onto the inked surface of the stamp. We then glued a birdhouse charm onto the lower portion of the domino using E6000 glue. We added some beads and spacers to our gold cord, and applied gold leafing to the edges of the tile to finish the piece.

Leaf Pendant

We swabbed Colorbox chalk ink directly on the top sides of our domino to give the smooth surface a feathery appearance. (The center was left uncolored to accent the green leaves.) We used the same ink to stamp the leaves. We inked a stipple image stamp and lightly kissed it over the stamped leaves. We swabbed the domino edges with a coordinating color of chalk ink and heat-set.

Kokopelli Pin

We applied chalk ink directly to the domino and muted the color by rubbing with an alcohol-moistened swab. We used a darker ink to edge the surface and frame our image and then heat-set the colors. We stamped a Kokopelli image on the tile, and used a copper Sharpie marker to accent the stamp and add hand-drawn dots and swirls. We also used the marker to color the edges of the domino. We then heat-set the colors and attached a pin back with E6000 glue.

Blue Beaded Tile

We marbled the domino with blue ink and a silver leafing pen, and heat-set the inks. We stamped our image and heat-set it. We placed small drops of Diamond Glaze clear adhesive on the "buds" of our tree and used a tweezers to set black seed beads into the adhesive. We let the adhesive dry, and then accented the edges of the domino with a silver leafing pen.

Maiden Pin

We edged our domino with chalk ink and heat-set the ink. We inked only the portion of our large stamp that would fit on the surface of the domino, set the stamp on its back, and pressed the domino onto the inked portion of the stamp. We heat-set the image and applied a pin back with E6000 glue.

Gifts for *Giving*

Use your favorite rubber stamps to make an elegant throw pillow for the holiday season.

This super-simple technique lets you create your own holiday pillows for less than $20. That makes these attractive little items perfect for gift giving—or for adding to your own home for a splash of holiday cheer!

You Will Need

- ½ yard polyester/rayon velvet
- Measuring tape
- Rubber stamps (large, open designs work best)
- Spray starch
- Iron and cotton press cloth
- Scissors, pins, marking pencil, matching thread
- ¾ yard decorative trim
- Polyester batting or appropriate pillow insert

Optional:
- Beads

1 NOTE: Since not all velvets respond to this technique the same way, try Steps 1 and 2 on a piece of scrap velvet to determine ironing time and to test your results before stamping your pillow.

Cut two 14- by 18-inch pieces of velvet. Find and mark the center on the wrong side of one velvet piece.

Measure the dimensions of the stamp you will be using for the center of your pillow. Transfer these measurements to the wrong side of the fabric to help you center the stamp in the middle of the pillow.

2 Place your stamp rubber side up on a flat, hard surface. Place the right side of the velvet facedown over the rubber stamp, centering the stamp inside your markings.

Spray a small, even amount of spray starch over the area to be embossed.

Cover the velvet with a press cloth and press with a hot, dry iron, holding the iron in place for about 10 to 12 seconds.

After this, carefully lift the iron away from the surface without dragging the iron across the fabric.

4 Pin beaded trim to the side edges of the pillow. Sew in place. With right sides together, place the back panel of the pillow over the front and sew in place using ½-inch seam allowance. Leave a 6- to 8-inch opening to stuff the pillow.

Turn right side out.

3 OPTIONAL: You can highlight your embossed pillow design by adding a few glittering beads here and there around the edge or center of your embossing. To do this, double-thread a needle and sew on the beads the same way that you would sew on a button.

5 Stuff the pillow with batting, making it as firm as you wish. (Generally, decorative pillows are stuffed fairly firmly.)

Hand sew the opening closed.

Card Art

Have a stack of leftover holiday cards? Turn them into a piece of 3-D art.

Greeting cards sold in packs are the basis for this clever piece of art. The repeating images can be cut and layered to create a scene with depth and beauty.

(After-Christmas sales are a good time of year for this project, but I keep my eye out all year long for any cards that will make a nice presentation.)

You Will Need

- 6 (or more) of the same greeting card
- Decorative frame
- Fine-point pen (black)
- X-acto knife and cuticle scissors
- 3M Mounting Tape*
- Tacky Glue
- Paper adhesive
- Scissors

Optional:
- Colored card stock

* Mounting tape is a thin layer of foam with adhesive on both sides. The foam separates the different layers of the picture just enough to add dimension.

1 Select the cards you want to use. Pictures that have depth are the best choice for this project. Look for pictures that have images stacked in front of other images, such as a Christmas tree with many packages, an open doorway looking into a house, or rows of houses in a town. Landscapes and cityscapes work especially well. The more layers you use, the more interesting your finished picture will be.

Find a frame for your finished picture that is as close in size to your card as possible. If the card you choose is slightly larger than the opening, you can trim it to size before you cut out the design areas. If you choose a card that is a bit smaller than the frame opening, attach the final stack of cards to a backing sheet that is the correct size for the frame.

Look for a frame that has as much depth as possible since your finished stack of cards will be fairly tall.

2 Use one of your cards as a planning card. With a black fine-tip pen, outline the different areas of the picture—trees, houses, sky, mountains, and so on. Some greeting card pictures extend to the edges of the card, while others are framed within the perimeter. If you are working with a card that has a frame, you can cut the frame away completely, or work within the frame. For this card, the front piece is just an empty frame cut from an extra card.

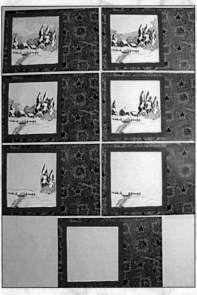

4 Use an X-acto knife or a cuticle scissors for cutting the cards.

Cut away the greeting portion of each card, leaving only the picture. It is easiest to work from back to front when cutting the design areas. The last card in the stack will remain whole. Label each of the cards on the back as you finish cutting them to avoid confusion later.

The more you work toward the foreground, the more of the picture will be cut away.

3 Decide which areas you want to be on the same plane in your picture and number them accordingly. Start with the foreground. In our example, the road, the fence, and the meadow are on the same plane—and all No. 1's.

No. 2 images are two of the tall trees, the land in front of the buildings, and the second part of the road leading to the farm buildings.

No. 3 has the buildings and the remaining trees, and so on.

The sky is the final plane in our example and is marked number 6. Each plane needs a separate card cut according to the plan. If you have six planes, you need six cards.

It may be helpful to do a drawing of each cutout using tracing paper to outline each of the areas to be cut away. Use these as a guide when cutting.

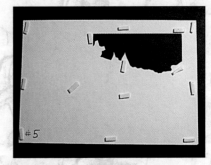

5 Use double-faced mounting tape to attach the cards to one another.

Lay your last card faceup on the table. Flip the next card on its face and place small pieces of mounting tape along the cut-out edges, the outer edges, and in the center of the card to give support. Remember that small objects such as street lamps, small trees, and people need to be supported with their own piece of mounting tape. Remove the paper backing on the tape, line up the card carefully with the one below it, and place it. Repeat for all the cards.

Clean the glass in your frame and insert the stack for a test fit. If the piece is too small, cut a piece of card stock to the actual size of the opening and use that as a background. Replace glass and backing.

Holiday *Events*

Sprinkle some personal flavor on your holiday events when you try a new holiday craft! Start with a holiday card project—this one is complete with a list of questions to consider before you begin creating. And don't forget to deck the halls … with crisp and clever glass bulbs; handsome, hand-stitched ornaments; or an elegant Victorian-style stocking.

For shining celebrations, turn to the candle ideas that follow. You will find candle decorations and centerpieces from cozy-and-charming to rich-and-resplendent. Every project here will help make all your holiday events light, bright and merry!

Handmade Holiday Greetings

This year, show your friends and family your creative side by whipping up a batch of truly personal holiday cards.

aking personal holiday cards are a snap with a little planning and some fun ideas.

Consider your budget and the amount of time you want (or have) to spend on them. For instance, embossing and hand coloring are beautiful touches, but do you want to tackle that alone on 75 cards?

To remove any anxiety and improve the creativity on your handmade cards, start early.

If you will have help making the cards, consider an idea that will allow the whole family to take part. An assembly line can offer efficiency and can allow everyone to lend a hand on one step or another. Even young children can stick stamps on envelopes or lick them shut. And while computer-addressed envelopes definitely speed up the process, remember that a hand-addressed envelope sends a very sincere wish.

SPECIAL PROJECT TIP

• Before you cut all your components for the cards you will be making, complete one sample card. This will ensure that your measurements are accurate and you don't need to fine-tune anything.

1 This self-closing card with a paper "buckle" starts from a 5½- by 11-inch piece of card stock.

Fold the outside, short sides of the card in at the 4¼- and 8½-inch points to create the card body. To make folding easier, score along these points with the scoring blade on your paper cutter or with a stylus or dull knife dragged along the edge of a ruler.

Stamp one side of your scored card stock. We used dye ink for stamping our images since it dries quickly, cleans up easily, and is available in many color choices.

Once dry, fold the card so that the shorter side is on top.

2 Cut a small square of coordinating card stock slightly larger than your charm, and stick the charm to the square using Zots large clear adhesive dots. Place the paper square in the center of your card front (this is the larger flap) and glue it down.

3 Using a craft knife and ruler, cut around three sides of the "buckle," leaving the side toward the fold intact. We left a ⅛-inch border around the punched square for emphasis.

Our card features a metal snowflake charm used as an accent for our buckle.

SPECIAL PROJECT TIP

• Shop around for paper options when making a number of cards. Some papers are much less expensive than others, and will provide a similar look for a lot less. A standard 8½- by-11-inch sheet of paper cut in half lengthwise will make two cards that can be placed in a standard A2-size envelope and will also each accommodate a 3- by 5-inch photo.

4 Fold the card closed and crease well. Pop the "buckle" up slightly (a) and slip the shorter side under the flap to secure your card (b).

To finish your card, stamp an appropriate greeting on the inside of your card, or create a matted version by layering coordinating colors of card stock and then stamping your greeting on the top layer.

While you have your ink and stamps out, keep in mind that an accent or two stamped on the front or back of the envelope is a nice touch.

Creative *Candles*

Make a special occasion unique by adding a personal sentiment to a tea light candle shade.

You can light up your life (or your living room) with beautifully handcrafted shades for tea light candles. You can customize your candles to match your decor or a party theme, and you'll find these are perfect accents for an extra-special touch on any occasion.

You Will Need

- Translucent vellum
- Scraps of colored card stock
- Paper cutter or ruler and scissors
- Rubber stamps
- Permanent ink pad in a dark color (we used black StazOn)
- Colored markers
- Double-sided tape
- Metal eyelets and setting tools
- ⅛-inch hole punch
- Ribbon or narrow cording
- Decorative scissors (optional)
- Glass votive candleholders and tea lights

SPECIAL PROJECT TIP

• As with any candle, never leave these decorations unattended. Use only with a heavy glass votive holder and a small tea light. Make sure that any ribbon or other material used in these shades does not come near the candle itself.

1 These decorative candle shades are made of two pieces of vellum and two pieces of coordinating card stock.

Cut two strips of scrap card stock to measure about 1 by 7 inches. (You can stamp the center of these strips with a sentiment or leave it blank.) Cut two pieces of vellum 7 inches long and as tall as the glass votive you plan to use. (Ours were about 3 inches tall by 7 inches long.)

Lay the vellum on your work surface. Stamp an image in the upper two-thirds of the center of the vellum using permanent ink and allow it to dry. For a raised image, you can use pigment ink to stamp an image on the upper two-thirds of one or both sheets; sprinkle embossing powder over the image, and use a heat tool to melt the powder. NOTE: Vellum can blister if it comes in direct contact with the heat tool. Be careful to keep the tip of the heat tool moving over the image. As soon as the powder melts in one area, move to the next section of your image.

2 Flip your stamped or embossed sheet of vellum over and color the image from the back. Don't worry if your marker strays slightly over the lines; it will be muted on the front of the sheet when it is flipped back over. Coloring from the back will give your image a stained glass look. Allow the marker to dry completely before you assemble your votive cover. TIP: For a bolder statement, use dark gray or black pigment ink and embossing powder to mimic the leaded veins of a stained glass window. A metallic color also works well.

SPECIAL PROJECT TIP

• You can vary the look of this project in several ways. Simply punch several holes or set several eyelets in each side of the vellum and lace your ribbon through like a shoelace.

Or make a cylindrical sleeve for a votive holder by simply wrapping the vellum around the glass and overlapping it in the back. Secure with brads or eyelets and laced ribbon.

You could also form a shade-like cover for a wine glass and place your tea light in the glass for an elevated votive. (This is really pretty if you use a decorative scissors on the curved edges!) Finally, experiment with different-colored vellum, or vellum with glitter or botanical inclusions.

3 Using double-sided tape, attach the paper border along the bottom of your stamped vellum sheets. Make sure to use enough tape so that you don't end up with gaps between the card stock and the vellum. A solid strip of tape along the top edge works best.

Place the two sheets of vellum together, with the stamped images facing out. Punch a small hole along each of the shorter sides of the two sheets, centering it about ¾ of an inch in from the edge. Place an eyelet in each hole and set it to secure the two sheets together. (Make sure that you set both of the eyelets so that they are oriented in the same direction.) String a length of ribbon or cording through the eyelets and tie a bow, being careful not to let the ribbon or any of your other materials extend over the top of the holder or near the votive inside.

Personal *Style*

Want to create a treeful of inexpensive ornaments in less than an hour? Try one of these clever tricks.

We started with a dozen clear glass balls, which we purchased at our local hobby store. (You can buy a dozen of these for less than $10.)

These ornaments are intended to serve as creative canvases. Several easy ways to decorate these include painting or embellishing them with glitter or stickers or faux stained glass.

However, we decided to try something a little different. In several cases, we decided to take advantage of the glass itself by adding our decorative details on the inside. The tops of the ornaments slip off easily—but watch for sharp edges—so you can then "decorate" the inside. The possibilities are endless, but we only have room to include two ideas for adding interest to our unique ornaments.

Beads and Tassels

To make an extra-elegant ornament, you can embellish the outside of your decoration. We did this using a product called Terrifically Tacky Tape and some super-small glass marbles, both of which we found at our local craft store. The Tacky Tape is extremely sticky, double-sided tape that let us create a pattern on the outside of the ornament. We then removed the protective backing from the tape, exposing the second sticky side. We placed a few spoonfuls of the tiny glass marbles in a saucer and then pressed them into the tape.

Gold and Silver Cord

This ornament uses inexpensive gold and silver cord in a free-form shape inside the glass for plenty of sparkle. We simply cut two pieces of cord about 12 inches long, one each of silver and gold. Use a pencil or chopstick to poke the free ends of the cord inside the ornament, and let the cords relax into a free-form shape. Tuck in the other cut ends, and replace the ornament top.

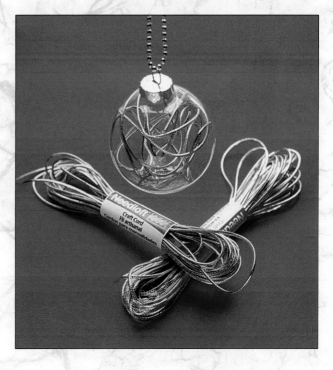

Vintage Christmas Ornaments

Turn classic old images into charming decorations.

Vintage postcards have a unique charm, with sweet images of days gone by. In general, published items that were first printed more than 95 years ago are copyright free, meaning that you don't need to pay the creator to reuse the image. Taking advantage of that fact, we created three unique Christmas ornaments by transferring the designs from three old postcards to fabric, and then added our own embellishments.

Embellishing fabric is a fun way to create in that you can add as much or as little detail as you like. Depending on your image, you can embellish fabric transfer ornaments with satin ribbon, silk embroidery ribbon, embroidery floss, metallic ribbon, and a wide variety of decorative beads and sequins.

Although we used vintage postcards for our designs, you can find a number of ready-to-print, copyright free images available on CDs from a variety of retailers. Check your local craft store, or search online for "Copyright Free Christmas Image CD".

You Will Need

- Fabric image printed on muslin, embellished in a style of your choice (See examples at left for ideas)
- Rotary cutter, mat, and ruler
- ½ yard muslin (will make several ornaments)
- Pellon
- Cotton batting
- 1/16-inch satin ribbon
- Sharp scissors

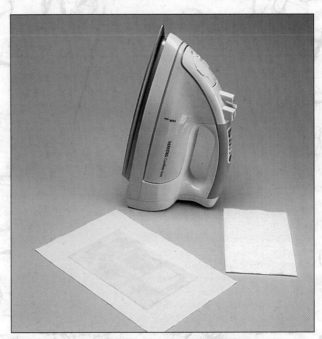

1 Transfer the images you've selected to fabric by printing them from a computer onto special fabric-backed paper. Once you've embellished your particular fabric transfer as you like (see our images and how we embellished them at left for a few suggestions), you can create a quilted backing to finish the piece.

Use a rotary cutter, mat, and ruler to trim your transfers from the fabric-backed muslin, leaving as much space around each as possible.

2 Measure the printed design area of each transfer. Cut a piece of Pellon and cotton batting slightly smaller than each transfer. Set aside the cotton batting. Iron one piece of the Pellon to the back of each transfer. Do not overlap printed design area.

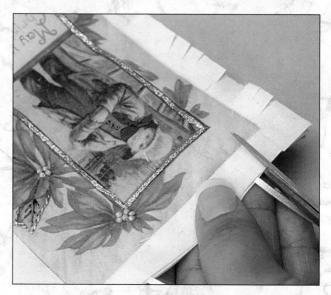

3 Use the rotary cutter to trim the muslin, leaving a $\frac{1}{2}$-inch muslin border on all four sides.

Using the cut cotton batting piece, sew one piece to the back of your transfer. Take a couple of small stitches going through any worked embroidery thread on the back side of the transfer to anchor the batting.

Measure transfers (border included) and cut two additional pieces of muslin backing for each. (When sewn together, each ornament will have three pieces of muslin for a thicker fringe.)

Pin two pieces of muslin to the back of each transfer. Cut a 10-inch piece of $\frac{1}{16}$-inch satin ribbon for the hanger. Place ribbon between the muslin layers and pin in place. Sew along muslin border, staying close to the outer edge of the printed transfer.

4 Using a small, very sharp scissors, clip around the border every $\frac{1}{4}$ inch. Clip up to the stitched line, being careful not to cut through it. Clip straight sides first. Clip the corners inward, as you would cut a pie.

Wet the tips of your clean fingers using cold water. Lightly run your wet fingers back and forth across one clipped side of the ornament at a time until the edges are slightly wet. You will see the clipped edges start to fluff. When the edges are damp but not soaked, place the ornament in a clothes dryer on low heat for 3 to 4 minutes. Remove from the dryer; if necessary, straighten corners and hang to finish drying.

French Knot

Bring the needle up, turning the needle so it points toward your left arm. Wrap the thread twice around the needle so it is snug but not tight. Hold the loose end of the thread with your opposite hand, turn the needle toward your heart, and take the needle down into the fabric at 2. Let the loose thread you are holding slide through your fingers until it all goes to the back of the fabric. Continue in this manner until all the knots are in place.

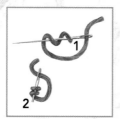

Figure 1

Stem Stitch

Keep the thread on the lower side of the needle, working the stem stitch along the drawn line. Bring the needle up at 1 and down at 2. Needle comes up at 3 halfway between 1 and 2. Continue in this manner until area is completed.

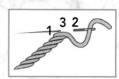

Figure 2

Ribbons and Beads

For our little boy ornament, we used a 6-inch piece of deep red silk ribbon to create a scarf around his neck. We used embroidery floss to work three French knots (fig. 1), on the boy's shirt. We used ⅛-inch gold ribbon to outline the frame around the boy by placing the braid over the frame area. (When working with braid, be sure the braid lies flat and smooth. If needed, use your fingers to turn the braid where it goes down into fabric so it lies flat.) We sewed on yellow green and buttercup beads, filling in the centers of the poinsettias on the right side of the transfer.

We then used the stem stitch (fig. 2) and one strand of floss to stitch the veins of the leaves and to outline the leaves on the right side of the transfer.

Embroidered Accent

To embellish our lady image ornament, we placed a single bead in the center of the snowdrops at the top of the transfer. We used the stem stitch (fig. 2) and one strand of peach floss to outline the rim and bow of her bonnet. We worked the lacing on her dress using peach floss by starting at the bottom and working one half of the lacing up to the top. We worked the crossover lacing back down to her waist.

We added additional beads just under the outlined bow, working over the flower cluster, and added other beads in the centers of the holly branches.

Embroidered Design

For this piece, we used the stem stitch (fig. 2) with one strand of light green floss to work the stem and branches, and used white sewing thread to sew on sequins underneath beads.

The Holidays
by Candlelight

Take advantage of the warm light candles bring to any festivity with these clever ideas.

Candles deserve a special place in every home—and more so than ever during the holiday season. These elegant flickering lights can make even the most mundane snack seem wonderful, but pair can-dles with an elegant meal for two or 20 and you'll have created an event.

Here are a few ideas to get you started and a couple of commonsense reminders: All candles need supervision. Don't leave a room with a candle burning in it, and keep an eye on pets, children, and guests to make sure that these beauties don't get tipped over. Place your candles in a spot where they will be safe, and enjoy!

You Will Need

- 3 heavy-glass bud vases
- Masking tape or painter's tape in a variety of sizes
- Access to a sink and running water
- Safety glasses
- Rubber gloves
- Etching cream
- Plastic plate
- Paintbrush

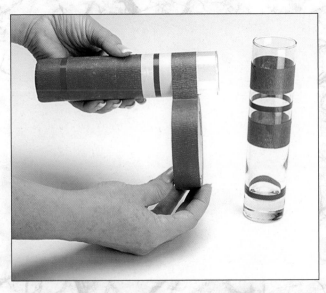

1 We added a simple striped pattern to our bud vases to make them a bit more elegant. We did this by making a pattern using a variety of widths of masking and painter's tape.

NOTE: Begin by taping the entire glass to keep your etching lines clean and straight later on. We taped ours like this:

We started with a 1-inch piece of tape at the bottom of the vase, followed by ¼-inch tape, 2-inch tape, ½-inch tape, ¼-inch tape, ½-inch tape, and finished with a piece of 1-inch tape.

Decide which sections of the vase you wish to etch, and then remove the bands of tape on those areas only.

2 Put on safety glasses and rubber gloves and work on a pro-tected surface.

With paintbrush, apply a thick, consistent layer of etching cream on the exposed areas of your vase, brushing from side to side and up and down over the vase. Be careful not to get any etching cream inside the vase.

Leave the etching cream on for about 5 minutes, then wash it off with water. Remove the remaining tape, and clean the vase thoroughly.

TIP: We displayed taper candles in our bud vases. To keep the taper candles in place, we applied a small dab of hot glue to the bottom of the candle before placing it inside. Drip-free candles work best for this setup.

Cinnamon Splendor

We purchased an inexpensive, unpainted, wood shelf from our local craft store. (Select a shelf that is wide enough to accommo-date a heat-resistant glass saucer that will hold your pillar can-dle.) Paint the shelf in a shade of your choice, then use a number of broken cinnamon sticks to frame the shelf around the front and sides. Attach the sticks with liberal dabs of hot glue. Place the heat-resistant saucer inside the shelf, and place a pillar candle inside. Important: The candle must not come into contact with the shelf or the cinnamon sticks. If you light this candle, replace it when it has burned to within 2 inches of the top of the sticks. (This decoration is actually pretty enough to stand on its own without lighting the candle.)

You Will Need

- One large terra cotta saucer (we used a 14-inch one)
- Clear acrylic sealer
- Base spray paint (we used a rich crimson)
- Gold "glitter" craft paint and brush
- 1-inch blue painter's tape
- Metallic gold spray paint
- Clear glass votives and tea lights

1 Thoroughly spray the terra cotta saucer with an acrylic sealer. (This will help your base paint adhere cleanly to the porous saucer.) Let dry.

Follow this with a coat of your selected base color. Let dry.

2 Once your base coat has dried, use a 1-inch brush to liberally apply gold glitter craft paint. This paint has a clear base and contains gold flecks in it. This will give you a shimmering effect across your saucer.

Art from Your Yard

One of the easiest—and most inexpensive—ways to add a little holidays cheer with candles is to use a clear glass cylinder and a floating candle. Place a few bits of greenery from your yard—we used snips of an arborvitae and a couple of pine cones—inside the vase, and fill it with water. Place your floating candle on top. You can arrange a bit more greenery around the outside of the base. Tie a few jingle bells on a piece of gold cord and loop this around the outside of the vase for a bit more glitter.

A Candy Cane Candleholder

This candleholder is easy to make and looks lovely with a glass votive and tea light inside. Purchase two small unpainted wooden bases at your local craft store and paint them in a color of your choice. Using a hot-glue gun, glue the two bases together to form a platform at least 2 inches high.

Take eight candy canes and glue two canes together back to back with hot glue. Repeat until you have four sets of two. Then simply glue these canes to your bases. Hold them for a moment until the glue sets, and then place a small glass votive with a tea light inside.

3 Make a geometric design across the inside and edges of your saucer with blue painter's tape. (The portions of the saucer that are covered will retain their base color after the next step.)

Spray over the saucer with gold spray paint. You can spray the entire piece heavily or spray lightly to leave a more mottled appearance. Let dry. Remove the painter's tape to expose the design on the red base color beneath. Fill the saucer with a variety of clear glass votives and tea lights.

A Victorian *Christmas*

This oh-so-elegant stocking can be made from sumptuous remnant fabrics and a bit of old costume jewelry!

Making your own Christmas stocking can be a pleasure when you work with smaller pieces of remnant fabrics that may be too expensive for larger projects. We used an old-fashioned brocade and a piece of washed silk to make this lovely decoration.

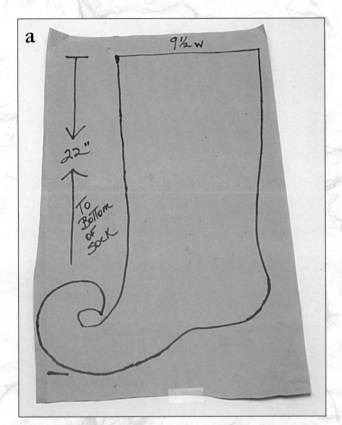

1 We created our own pattern for this stocking in a style similar to ones we had seen in old books. We used a large piece of brown paper, lightly sketching out our design until we were pleased with the shape (a). Our finished pattern was about 22 inches tall and 9½ inches wide. (TIP: This stocking has a curled toe. When you create your pattern, make sure that the toe is at least 2 inches wide at the tip, since this will allow ample room for your seam allowances, and enough room to turn the piece right side out after stitching.)

Once you're satisfied with your pattern, cut two pieces of fabric for the stocking.

Then measure the width across the top of your stocking pattern. To create the cuff, cut a fabric rectangle double the width of the top of the stocking by 10 inches long (b). (For example, our stocking measured 9½ inches across the top, so we cut our rectangle 19 inches wide by 10 inches long.) Cut two. (One is for finishing interior of stocking. See Steps 6 and 7.)

2 Hand sew loose pearls randomly on the right side of your front stocking pattern piece. Sew the pearls on as you would a button: double thread a needle and double knot the end. Insert the needle from the wrong side of the fabric through to the front. Pass the needle through the pearl and then back through the fabric. Repeat and secure with a knot. Add as many pearls as you like. NOTE: Keep pearls at least 1 inch in from the raw edge of the fabric.

3 With right sides of the stocking pieces together, pin the front of the stocking to the back. Sew together using ½-inch seam allowance, leaving the top edge open. Turn right side out. NOTE: If your stocking has a pointed toe as ours does, trim fabric close to the stitching at the toe to help the pieces lie flat.

4 Fold one cuff in half along the length, right sides together, and stitch ends together using ½-inch seam allowance. Press seam open.
   Turn the cuff right side out and fold in half, lining up the raw edges.

5 Slip the cuff over the top of the stocking. Pin the cuff to the stocking, lining up the raw edges and seams. Sew in place using ½-inch seam allowance.

6 Finish one edge of the second, interior cuff along the length with a ½-inch double hem. Fold cuff in half along the length, right sides together, and stitch ends together using ½-inch seam allowance. Press seam open. Slip the cuff over the top of the stocking and pin the cuff to the stocking, lining up the raw edges and seams. Sew in place using ½-inch seam allowance.

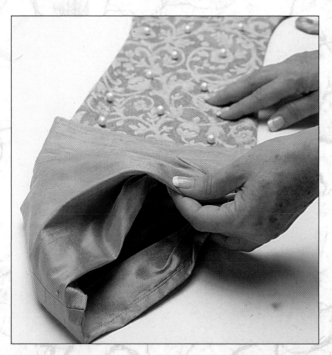

7 To finish the interior cuff, trim away excess fabric at the top of the stocking to about ¼ inch from the stitching. Turn the cuff right side out and slip the cuff into the stocking. Press the top edge of the stocking to make the seam lie flat.

8 Pin decorative trim around the top edge of the stocking and sew in place. Turn end of trim under to conceal the raw edge and prevent it from fraying.

SPECIAL PROJECT TIP

• If you create a stocking with a curled toe, as we did, stuff the end of the finished stocking with some polyester batting to help the stocking keep its shape. This will also help it hang better because of the added weight at the bottom of the stocking.

9 Remove the clasp from a string of costume jewelry pearls. (You'll need to use a necklace that is knotted between each bead so that your string doesn't unravel.)

Using a double threaded needle, hand sew one string of pearls to the top edge of the stocking, keeping the stitches between the pearls. (NOTE: You don't need to sew in between each pearl. We found that sewing between every third or fourth pearl was sufficient.) Repeat along the bottom edge with two more rows.

OPTIONAL: You can stitch a small chair tassel tie to the top of your stocking from which to hang the stocking, or add a loop of ribbon for the same purpose.

Classic *Decorating*

Do your home décor daydreams feature trompe l'oeil textures, dashing draperies, or a rich and formal dining room? Here we demonstrate faux painting methods you can use to add depth and texture to your walls. Dress up your windows with one of several stylish tieback techniques. And for your dining room, discover more than a half dozen projects that add life and luxury to tired chairs, an old light fixture, or a plain ceiling or wall. Add a touch of class to your home and make your daydreams come true!

Pro Faux

Easy faux finishes to freshen your walls

Changing the color of a room with paint is one of the most popular projects you can do yourself. Faux finishing, a form of painting with "layers" of color, is a project within the reach of any do-it-yourselfer. While many readymade products are now available at any home improvement store to help you achieve a variety of faux finishes, you can also create your own using just paint, glaze, and a few household items.

This page shows six different faux finishes. You can see that the underlying colors you select for your faux finish will create a variety of results. On the next few pages, we'll show you three simple faux techniques, each of which can be varied to suit your own style. There is no right and wrong. If you like your end result, you've done your project well.

A few bits of advice before you start a faux finishing project: Consider the mood you want your room to reflect. A well-done faux finish can create a real "atmosphere" in any space. The colors you choose can inspire feelings of happiness (warm, sunny yellows), serenity (soft greens, pale blue grays), or warmth (golds, amber tones).

Whichever style you choose, always start by practicing the technique on a sample, or several samples, to test your color combinations and to make sure you're comfortable with the application process.

When doing a faux finish, be sure to get your paint into the corners using smaller brushes, sponges, or rags, working the paint to the edge. In some situations, you can also tape off the adjoining wall to keep the edge clean. Keep a neat ceiling line by taping off the ceiling and touching up any seepage with ceiling paint. Tape off your woodwork and protect your floors and furniture. Take all the precautions you would normally use when beginning a painting project.

And finally, just a note: You'll find that faux finishing is messier than plain painting, especially when you're mixing several shades of paint with the same brush, but the results will be stunning!

Three-color Blend

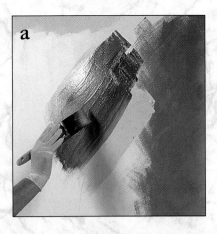

a

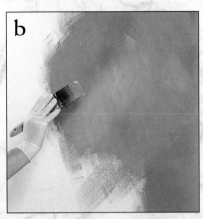

b

1 This technique consists of placing several brushstrokes of different colored paints on a wall, and then blending the shades together with a brush dipped in glazing medium. Working in a small area at a time, apply several brush strokes of your three colors fairly close together on the wall (a). Immediately dip your brush in the glaze mixture and start blending the colors together (b). You don't want to blend so much that your three colors turn into one color, but blend enough so that they make an interesting pattern. It really couldn't be easier! If you don't like the way an area looks after it dries, you can go back and reapply more paint and use additional glazing liquid to help blend it.

SPECIAL PROJECT TIP

• An easy way to keep your paints handy for this project is to invest in a plastic tote that will hold four quart cans—three of paint, and one for glaze. This also keeps drips to a minimum.

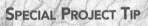

Bagging Technique

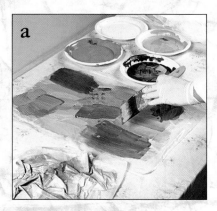

a

b

3 Lay one piece of plastic down on a paint-proof surface. Paint several strokes of each color paint onto the plastic, crisscrossing the strokes as you work. Add a stroke or two of the glazing medium to help the colors blend a bit. Fold the plastic, set it aside and repeat the process until you have 10 pieces of plastic prepared.

You Will Need

- Three shades of latex paint in an eggshell or satin finish: a light, medium, and dark color in the same family.
- A roll of tall plastic kitchen garbage bags (the cheaper, the better)
- Scissors
- Brushes
- Glazing medium

1 This technique looks best when the base coat of the wall is a pale, neutral color, or if you first paint your walls using the palest shade of paint from the three you've selected.

2 This technique uses a lot of trash bags. Cut off the sealed end of the bags; open them up, and cut them in half so you end up with two large pieces of plastic. Start with about 20 bags for a medium-sized room.

4 Open up a bag and lightly touch the bag to the wall. It will adhere because of the paint. Lightly brush your fingers over the bag and pull away. Continue to lift and press the bag, turning as you go, continuing until you're unable to lift and apply any more paint. Move to the next area, open another bag, and repeat, repeat, repeat.

Sponging Layered Glazes

You Will Need

- Glazing medium
- Three complementary light-to-medium shades of latex paint
- Large sea sponge
- Plastic plates
- Containers for glazes
- Newspapers

SPECIAL PROJECT TIP

• You'll find that natural sea sponges come in a variety of shapes and textures. Experiment until you find the shape that works best for you.

1 This technique looks best when the base coat on the wall is a pale, neutral color.

2 The secret to this technique is to make sure the colored glazes you will be sponging on are transparent. To make the glaze, mix 1 part paint to 5 parts glaze and stir well. Repeat in separate containers for all three colors. You want a transparent color after mixing; if any of your paints are extremely dark, add more glazing liquid to that mix.

Dampen a sea sponge with water and wring it out extremely well.

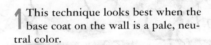

3 Begin working with the darkest glaze you've created. Pour some of the glaze onto a plastic plate. Dip the sea sponge into the glaze, and then gently tap the sponge on an extra paper plate to remove any excess glaze before lightly wiping the sponge across the wall. The sponge should be rotated and redipped in the glaze from time to time. Wipe the entire room with the darkest glaze. Once you've done this, repeat, using the second darkest glaze, and finish the room with a third coat, this time with the lightest shade.

Simply *Elegant*

Versatile window treatments are a snap when you turn two sheer panels into up to 10 different looks.

Changing the appearance of your windows can be a surprisingly easy task when you use materials on hand in different ways to create varied looks.

In this case, we found a way to turn two different-colored sheer panels—one cream and one sage green—into up to 10 different looks, simply by rearranging how we placed the curtains on our window. We used a double curtain rod (see Special Project Tip on next page) to enable us to hang both panels on the same window. These rods are readily available at home improvement, bedding, and other stores. We then draped our window in different fashions, using decorative tiebacks to help us create several unique window treatments.

Before you start, a few tips: Fullness is important for any window treatment. When you're working with sheers, as we did, measure the width of your window and then multiply by three to determine whether you need one, two, or more panels to create a luxurious look. (For example, our window is 36 inches wide, so we need 108 inches of panel to allow proper draping.) One exception to this is lace sheers: Lace sheers show off their pattern best when you multiply the width of the window by 1½ or 2.

You Will Need

- Two (or more) sheer panels in different colors
- Double drapery rod
- Two decorative tiebacks
- Screwdriver
- Measuring tape
- Medium safety pins

Asymmetrical Tiebacks

To achieve this look, hang drapery rod at desired height and hang drapery panels on rods. Determine the desired height of your tiebacks. (As a rule of thumb, the bottom edge of the tieback should be at about one-third of the height of the window. For the best finished effect, never divide the window in half visually.

Here we have the tiebacks, each one-third of the way from the top or the bottom.

Alternative Looks:
For a different style, let the back panel hang free and tie back the front panel.

Graceful Tassel

To achieve this look, hang drapery rod at desired height and hang drapery panels on rods. Find the center of the front panel and gather fabric to desired height. Loop one side of the tieback in front of the panel and one behind, and fasten tieback ends together with safety pin. Measure to ensure that the tieback is in the middle of the window. Adjust folds in fabric to make tails even, and pull on back side of tieback to conceal the safety pin behind drapery rod.

SPECIAL PROJECT TIP

• Double drapery rods are easy to mount and let you hang two separate window treatments on one area. For this project, we used the double rod, two sheer panels, and two decorative tiebacks to create five different styles.

Opulent Valance

To achieve this look, hang drapery rod at desired height and hang drapery panels on rods. Measure in about 14 inches from outside edges on front panel. Loop one side of the tieback in front of the panel and one behind, and fasten tieback ends together with safety pin. Measure to ensure that tiebacks are equally spaced from the outside edge of the window.

Adjust the folds in the fabric to make tails even and pull on back side of tieback to conceal safety pin behind drapery rod.

SPECIAL PROJECT TIP

• If you reverse your panels, putting one color in front of another, you can get five additional looks with the same materials.

Comfortable *Dining*

This dining room went from drab and dreary to light and comfortable with the clever projects on the next few pages.

A little paint will hide a world of sins. That's one thing we confirmed for ourselves when we undertook this dining room redo. This comfortable room was depressingly drab, with its trim painted a murky brown that was anything but appetizing. In addition, while the room had many pretty details, its appearance was dated, and the whole space needed a facelift.

We started our project by removing some of the heavy furniture from the room. We decided to switch the unmatched table chairs with a set of secondhand "flea market finds" that we reupholstered and faux-painted. We created two "antique" pillars to serve as a focal point in the space, designed some new crystal lampshades, fashioned a gorgeous table centerpiece, added a few pretty accessories, and much more. You'll find out how you can do the same on the next few pages.

BEFORE

Cheery Chairs

We gave these old chairs new life by painting them, re-covering the cushions with new fabric, and adding simple pillows.

For some reason, it seems that old chairs accumulate over time. These cane-backed chairs had been sitting in a basement for quite a while, too good to throw, but too dated-looking to use. As part of our dining room makeover, we decided to give these chairs a facelift that brought them out of the basement into a prime location in our newly redone room.

Remaking dining room chairs is one of the easiest home decorating projects you can do. Don't be afraid to paint the chairs if their present appearance doesn't meet your needs. A good-quality primer followed with an attractive water-based enamel paint will give the pieces a new look and enough "wear and tear" durability to let them be used often.

The other parts of this project—re-covering the seat cushions and adding a small lumbar pillow—couldn't be simpler, either.

All you need is a staple gun, some new fabric, and perhaps some new foam and batting to give your own chairs a fresh appearance in an afternoon.

SPECIAL PROJECT TIP

• When choosing a fabric for such high-use items as chairs, pick one with good durability so that it will stand up to daily use and cleaning.

You Will Need

- Staple remover
- Needle-nosed pliers
- Scissors
- X-acto knife
- Upholstery batting (12 feet of 27-inch-wide batting is enough for 6 standard chair seats)
- 54-inch-wide decorative fabric (approximately 3 yards will cover 6 standard dining room chair seats)
- Staple gun and ⅜-inch and ½-inch staples

Optional:
- High-density foam
- Welting/Cording

1 If you have not previously done so, remove the seats from the chairs and set aside. (Mark each chair and seat with a corresponding number so you remember which seat goes where.)

Remove old fabric from each seat and transfer the number previously recorded to the wood base. (Since the chairs we were restoring had been stored in a basement for some time, we found that the staples had rusted in place, making them difficult to remove. Rather than struggle to remove the staples, we gently cut away the fabric with an X-acto knife and scissors. We then used our pliers to pry any remaining fabric out from under the staples.)

Remove any broken staples with the pliers or use a hammer to flatten the staples that cannot be removed.

Turn the seat platform over so that the staples are now hidden under the foam.

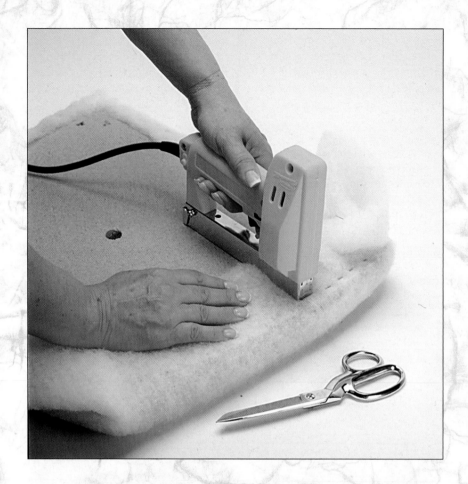

2 If you are working with fabric that is a plaid, stripe, or that has a distinctive pattern, mark the center of the seat platform at the top and bottom as well as the sides. This will be your guide to ensure that the fabric remains straight.

Measure the seat from bottom edge to bottom edge, over the foam in each direction, and add 4 inches; cut the batting and fabric equal to these dimensions. Place the batting on your work surface and center the seat on top. Starting at the center, front and back, bring the batting over the edge. Pull taut and staple in place, keeping staples about ½ inch apart. Repeat on the sides. Working from the center out to the corners, continue to staple the batting in place, stopping about 1½ inches from the corners. Fold the excess batting into a mitered corner at each corner and staple in place.

Trim excess batting.

3 Repeat the same procedure with the fabric as described in Step 2. Periodically turn the seat over and check to be sure that all edges are smooth, the fabric tension is even, and any patterns are straight.

Turn the seat to its back again, and insert additional staples. NOTE: These staples should almost touch each other.

Trim away excess fabric. If you wish, you can also add cording or welting to the edges of your seat for a more finished look, or you can leave them as they are.

Return seats to chairs.

How to Repaint a Chair

Remove the seats from all of your chairs and set aside. (Tip: Mark each chair and its seat with a corresponding number or letter, as the seats are probably not interchangeable, and the holes to reattach the seat will not always line up. So mark each chair and corresponding cushion No. 1, and so on.)

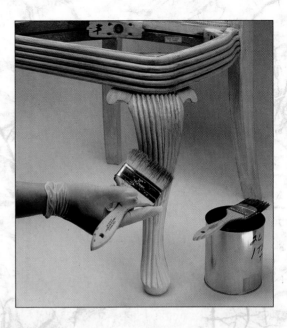

Wash the chair with TSP (a cleaning product found in hardware and paint supply stores) or wipe the chair down with a product called ESP/Liquid Sand (available at most home improvement stores). Either of these will remove any dirt or oily residue left over from old furniture polish.

After the chairs are clean and dry, apply one coat of a good quality primer (we used Zinsser) and then follow with two coats of acrylic satin-finish enamel paint. If you like, you can leave your chairs as they stand at this point, or you can add a faux finish to them, as we did next.

To give your chairs a warmer, "antiqued" appearance, mix 1 tablespoon of burnt umber tint with two cups of clear glaze.

Brush a thin layer of glaze on the chair, and feather it out with a chip brush. If the glaze is too thick, wipe off the excess with a wet rag. Be careful not to leave lines where you stop and start. Let the chair dry before reapplying glaze to any thin spots.

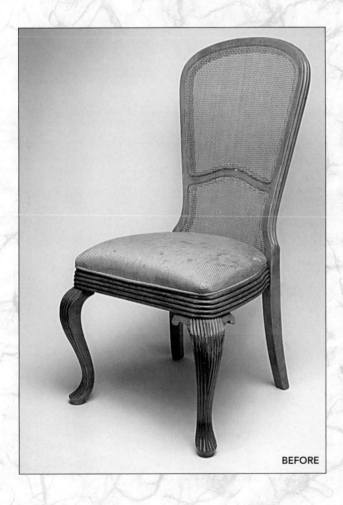

BEFORE

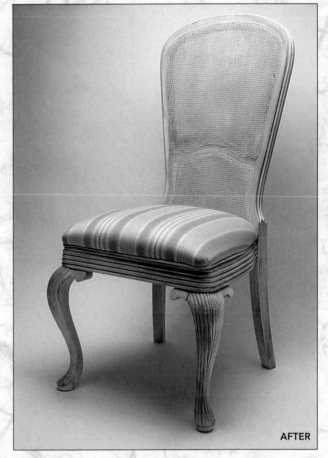

AFTER

A Relaxed *Meal*

Turn a standard linen napkin into a comfortable back pillow for a dining room chair.

This super-easy pillow offers perfect back support for a dining room chair. Better yet, since these little pillows are made from inexpensive dinner napkins, you can color coordinate your dining room tableware to match.

You Will Need

- Six (or more) 20- by 20-inch linen napkins
- Iron
- Pins
- Stitch Witchery (this is a fusible bonding used for hems and trims that is available at fabric stores)
- Scissors
- 20-ounce polyester fiberfill

Optional:
- Decorative iron-on appliques

Getting Started

Iron napkins to remove creases. Find the center of the napkin and mark with a pin. Measure 4 inches out from the center on both sides and mark with pins. Repeat on opposite end. Bring outside pins in toward the center, creating a box pleat, and press.

1 NOTE: The measurements here make a finished pillow 12 inches wide and 10 inches tall. You may need to adjust the size of your box pleat to fit the width of the back of your specific chair.

2 Open up the back side of the box pleat and place strips of the fusible bonding along the top and bottom edge, as well as the sides. Press in place following manufacturer's instructions. TIP: Keep the bonding tape as close to edges as possible.

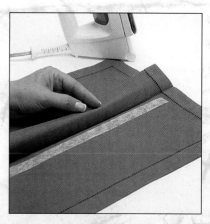

3 Lift up the edges on the front side of the box pleat and place a strip of bonding tape close to the inside of the folded edge on both sides of the box pleat. Press in place, following manufacturer's instructions.

4 OPTIONAL: Place decorative iron-on appliques on the front side of the napkin. Press in place following manufacturer's instructions.

5 Fold napkin in half, lining up the box pleat, and pin in place. Sew along the sides and top edge, leaving an opening along one side to stuff the pillow. TIP: Due to the thick edges of our napkin, we found it easier to keep our stitches close to the edge by installing the zipper/welting foot on our sewing machine.

6 Firmly stuff the pillow with the polyester filling, ensuring that all the corners are properly filled. Pin and sew the opening closed. If necessary, squeeze the pillow to adjust the filling.

A Crowning Touch

Turn a discarded picture frame into an elegant architectural detail on any ceiling.

One person's trash is another person's treasure. We've all heard that comment, and we couldn't agree more with the sentiment.

Consider this old picture frame that we found tucked away in an attic, ready to make its way to the discard pile. This long rectangular frame no longer held a picture, but the wood was solid and the shape was attractive.

It was too large for us to reuse as a frame—think of the old "sofa" pictures that used to hang in almost every living room—but we thought of a clever way to reuse it as a completely different decorative object.

We painted the frame the same color as the trim in our dining room; added some simple wood molding to

the edges, and then attached it to our ceiling to frame an existing chandelier. The whole process is quick and inexpensive (less than $20, excluding the frame), but we ended up with a unique architectural detail that looks as if it has always been part of this room.

You Will Need

- Lightweight wooden picture frame (select a frame at least 4 inches wider and longer than the ceiling base of your chandelier, or larger if you wish)
- ¾-inch decorative molding (enough to go around the inside dimensions of the frame)
- 1½-inch decorative molding (to go around the outside dimensions of the frame)
- Miter saw
- Measuring tape
- Paint primer designed for wood
- Acrylic paint (the same color as your ceiling)
- Wood glue
- Clamps
- Brad nails
- Stepladder
- A friend to help attach the molding
- Hammer
- Stud finder
- 3-inch nails
- Drill and bit
- Liquid Nails adhesive (construction grade)
- Awl
- Wood filler

SPECIAL PROJECT TIP

- We added painted stencils over and around our wooden frame after we had attached it to the ceiling for additional interest.

3 An extra pair of hands will be needed for Steps 3 and 4. Although you will be attaching the frame to the studs in your ceiling so that you will not be near electrical wiring, it's a good idea to turn off the electricity to the chandelier while you work, just as an extra safety measure.

Measure inside dimensions of the frame. Transfer these measurements to the ceiling in order to center the frame around the chandelier.

Locate studs with stud finder and mark location. Place frame against the ceiling and mark stud location on the frame. Pre-drill holes at these marks and insert 3-inch nails through your frame in preparation for the next step.

1 NOTE: We added lightweight wood molding to both the inside and outside edge of our picture frame so that the frame would fit tightly against our ceiling without any gaps. Depending on the frame you select, this may be optional.

Prime moldings and picture frame using good quality paint primer designed for wood. Using a miter saw, cut the ¾-inch molding to fit the inside dimensions of the frame, cutting corners at a 45-degree angle. Place a bead of wood glue along the inside edge of the frame and clamp in place until glue is dry.

2 Using a miter saw, cut 1½-inch molding to fit the outside dimensions of the frame, cutting corners at a 45-degree angle. Place a bead of wood glue along the top edge of the molding, press in place, and then nail in place using brad nails.

Paint the entire frame with two coats of paint the same shade as your trim.

4 Run a bead of Liquid Nails construction-grade adhesive around the entire perimeter of the frame. Center frame on previous markings and press in place. Hold in place for at least 2 minutes. TIP: Keep a damp cloth handy to wipe away any excess glue.

Hammer nails in place. Use an awl to countersink the nails. Fill nail holes with wood filler and touch up with paint.

SPECIAL PROJECT TIP

- Lightweight, premade wooden molding can be purchased in 8-foot sections at any home improvement store.

A Crowning Touch   **147**

Delightful *Details*

With a stencil and a few other items, you can create a raised plaster relief on any surface.

We wanted to add a bit of detail to the walls in our dining room, so we purchased two wall sconces from a local decorative accessory store. We repainted the sconces and then used an easy but elegant plaster treatment to created raised ivy garlands that seem to drape down our dining room wall.

You Will Need

- Ivy or grapevine stencil (we used a stencil called Flowing Ivy by Delta)
- Painter's tape
- Ready Mixed Patching
- Plaster (the quick-drying type)
- Putty knife
- Toothpicks
- Acrylic paints (we used
- shades of green, yellow, and white)
- Acrylic glaze
- Plastic plate
- Artist's brushes

1 Decide where you wish to place your sconces on the wall. Lightly mark the outer edges of the sconce with a pencil, and then remove. This will help with the placement of the stencil.

2 Tape the stencil in place. Using a putty knife, spread a thin layer of quick-drying plaster over the stencil. Immediately lift tape and gently remove the stencil. Rinse the excess plaster from the stencil, wipe it dry, and repeat. You can vary your stencil placement as you wish, since it is not important that the pattern be the same for each sconce.

3 After plaster has set for about 5 minutes, use a toothpick to lightly draw the veining details in the leaves. The toothpick should penetrate through to the wall in order to give depth to the detailing. Let plaster dry completely.

SPECIAL PROJECT TIP

• We loved the details on our sconces, but not the harsh gold color. To change their appearance, we painted them with one coat of good primer, and then added two coats of a pale cream paint that we also used on our trim in the room. We then used a variety of acrylic craft paints to pick out the details of the leaves, grapes, and vines. We let the sconces dry for two hours, and then wiped them down with a white-wash mixture to soften the effect. (Mix 1 part white craft paint to 2 parts glaze and enough water to give the mixture a cream-like consistency.) Lightly brush on the whitewash and then wipe or brush off the excess, leaving the whitewash in the relief.

4 Place a small dab of yellow, green, and white acrylic craft paint on a plastic or foam plate. Place a small amount of clear glaze on the plate as well. Dip your brush first in the glaze and then the paint (the glaze will make the paint a little more transparent). Paint the ivy, varying the colors of green and adding a little yellow or white from time to time to add depth and make the leaves look more natural. Let the paint dry completely before doing any touch-up work. NOTE: Each leaf doesn't have to look perfect. It is more natural looking to leave some leaves white to match the sconces above.

Center of Attention

This clever, reflective table centerpiece is made from an inexpensive dressing mirror.

Table centerpieces add a "finished note" to any dining room. We found a clever way to make a year-round centerpiece for this long rectangular table in only a couple of hours.

We purchased a standard-sized dressing mirror at our local discount store for about $10. We added a piece of wood backing, some very simple decorative wood trim (available at your local home improvement store), and some crystal drawer pulls for feet. Our materials cost less than $35, but you can make this project even more budget-friendly—$20 total—by substituting wooden ball feet for the crystal handles.

A little paint, and voilà!—you have an attractive centerpiece for any dining table that you can decorate for any season.

You Will Need

- One 12- by 48-inch dressing mirror with a wooden frame
- A piece of ¾-inch plywood cut ⅛ inch smaller than your mirror
- Measuring tape
- 1-inch screws
- Drill and bits
- Two 8-foot pieces of 1¼-inch decorative trim
- Miter saw
- Wood glue
- Hammer
- Finishing nails
- Primer
- Acrylic paint
- 6 crystal drawer pulls (you can find these at your local home improvement store)
- 1¾-inch wood screws
- Self-adhesive pads for bottom of feet (these will keep the crystal drawer pull feet from scratching your table)

Optional:
- Clear glaze
- Paint of your choice

SPECIAL PROJECT TIP

- Once you finish your mirror, there are many glazing techniques and products that can add a finishing touch to your tray. Consider applying a premixed metallic glaze or tint your own clear glaze with a bit of acrylic paint or stain. Choose an effect that coordinates with your decor.

We created an antiqued glaze for our mirror by mixing burnt umber tint with a clear glaze. Mix 1 tablespoon of burnt umber with 2 cups of clear glaze. Brush a generous coat of the glaze mixture onto the mirror frame and trim. Wipe off excess glaze with a soft cloth, leaving the glaze in the trim relief and frame of the mirror.

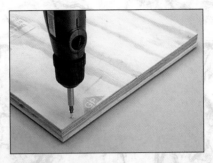

1 Measure the width and length of your mirror. Cut plywood ⅛ inch smaller than these measurements, so that the wood is just slightly smaller than the mirror frame. (You can have this wood cut to size at your local lumber store.)

To avoid splitting mirror frame, pre-drill eight holes—four on each long side—½ inch in from outside edge of your mirror frame. Attach plywood to the back of mirror frame using 1-inch wood screws. Keep screws ½ inch from edge. **TIP:** Before pre-drilling holes and attaching the frame, think about where you want the legs to sit (in the center of the frame, and each corner). Place your screws away from those areas so that you don't run into them when attaching the legs in Step 4.

3 Apply a bead of glue to the edge of the plywood and attach trim. At a few spots around your frame, use a drill to pre-drill a small hole through the trim, and then further secure the trim with a few finishing nails. (Pre-drilling ensures that you won't split your trim as you hammer in the nails.)

Apply two coats of acrylic paint to the frame of the mirror and the trim.

2 Using a good quality wood primer, paint both the wood trim and the mirror frame.

Place a piece of trim against the edge of the mirror frame and mark corners. Cut trim with a miter saw at a 45-degree angle to fit around the outside edges of the frame. (The trim will conceal the plywood and give the tray a nice finished edge.) Cut all four pieces of trim and dry fit around the mirror to make sure the pieces fit nicely.

4 Attach crystal handles to the bottom of the tray using 1¾-inch wood screws. Place a leg on each corner as well as one in the center of each side of the tray. Pre-drilling the holes for the screws will make it easier to install the drawer pulls.

Apply a self-adhesive vinyl bumper over the head of the screws to protect the table top. This will also prevent the tray from slipping on the table.

Luxurious *Lighting*

Embellish an old-fashioned crystal chandelier—or add glamour to any standard hanging light—with simple shades.

In this dining room, we were lucky enough to have an old-fashioned crystal chandelier already in place. However, as with many such chandeliers, the candle-style lights did not have shades. We decided to embellish this light by creating our own lead crystal shades, keeping with the style of the light.

We created five shades for $15 each in about an hour and a half. The crystal chains we used come in a variety of colors and sizes from a company called Freedom Crystal. Check the size of the bead you select for your particular size shade to ensure you order the necessary yardage.

Although we added these shades to a crystal chandelier, this project will work on any hanging light fixture—or even on a single lamp to which you want to add a little glamour.

Simply adjust the size or style of wire shade you select. You can also color-coordinate the wire shades to your particular light by spray painting them in a matching color. (For instance, if your chandelier is black, spray paint your shades black, or if it is gold, use a metallic gold to match.)

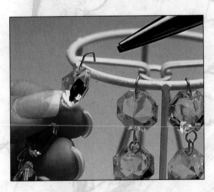

You Will Need

- Plain wire shade frames sized to fit your chandelier (We used five 5-inch-tall shades that were flared at the bottom to 6 inches. The top of the shade was 3 inches wide.)
- Primer spray paint
- Glossy spray paint
- 9 yards of 16 mm lead crystal beads
- Needle-nosed pliers or tweezers

Optional:
- Brass head pins

SPECIAL PROJECT TIP

- You can add a beautiful finishing touch to your shades by ordering an extra yard of crystal beads. Simply add one crystal bead to the bottom of each crystal bead chain length and let it dangle beneath the shade. If you would like more than one, order additional yardage. (There are about 75 beads in each yard of the 16 mm rope we used.)

BEFORE

1 Spray bare metal shades with one coat of primer and let dry. Follow with two separate coats of matching color and let dry.

Using a needle-nosed pliers or tweezers, pull one of the links open in the crystal bead chain. Straighten the pin with the pliers. Make a small hook in the end of the pin. Place the hooked pin over the top rim of the chandelier frame and squeeze the hook closed with the pliers.

2 Bring the crystal bead chain down to the bottom of the chandelier frame and pull open the link that is closest to the bottom of the frame. Repeat the same procedure as described in Step 1 to attach the crystal bead chain to the bottom of the shade.

For our flared 5-inch-tall shades, we were able to use a piece of crystal rope about 6 beads long. We put 12 strands of beads on each of our five shades. A slight droop in the crystal bead chain is fine and looks attractive.

SPECIAL PROJECT TIP

- Brass head pins can be handy when working on this project. These small jewelry-making supplies can be found in the jewelry and bead department at your local craft store.

You may find that it is sometimes difficult to straighten the pins on your crystal bead chain. If that happens, simply remove the crooked pin and insert a new one. Trim the pin to the desired length with the needle-nosed pliers.

Instant *Age*

Create these classic "antique" pillars with lightweight garden pots and a clever paint technique.

When professional interior designers consider the decor of a room, one of the things they evaluate is the focal points a particular space offers. These focal points—which are objects or details that catch the eye—are crucial for making a space appear warm and welcoming from the moment a visitor enters.

That philosophy lies behind the clever antique pedestals we created for this dining room.

At two points in the room, we were faced with a stretch of bare wall between our rearranged furniture. The space needed something, but whatever we chose needed to be tall enough to be seen, and decorative enough to add its own charm to the overall room.

We decided to create two faux antique pillars and then add an aged appearance to the pieces to make them look as if they've stood for ages in an English country garden. A patina is a finish that objects naturally acquire over time, as well as through the effects of erosion. The illusion of a patina finish can be created using acrylic paints, glazes, and wax.

To start, we purchased two plain plaster pedestals from our local hobby store and topped those with two lightweight garden pots designed for use outdoors. We were able to find both our pedestal and pot for around $30. We then tied these together visually with a clever paint technique and added a dried flower arrangement to each.

You Will Need

- Lightweight garden pot with raised relief details (our pot features grapes and leaves)
- Plaster pedestal
- Primer
- Two shades of acrylic paint—both a terra cotta or earth-toned base coat and very light grayish green top coat
- Glaze
- Chip brush
- Soft cloth or chamois
- Stencil brush
- Gloves
- Specialty paint products. (We purchased two specialty items at our local craft store—a copper-colored paint sold under the name Liquid Leaf and a colored wax sold under the name Treasure Gold.)

Optional:
- Burnt umber tint
- Glaze

1 Paint both the garden pot urn and the pedestal with a coat of good quality primer and let dry completely.

Once the urn and column are dry, paint both with a coat of the medium terra cotta base color. It is important that the pieces have an even coat of base color. (We applied two coats of the base color on the column due to the amount of texture in the plaster.)

Let dry.

2 Mix 1 part glaze with 1 part of the gray-green top color. Working in small sections, apply an even coat of the glaze mixture using the chip brush on the urn and column. Work the color into the raised relief portions of the urn and column. Move directly to Step 3.

3 While the glaze is still wet, wipe away excess glaze from the high points of the urn and column with a soft cloth or chamois. The glaze will dry quickly, so work in small areas. Let dry for at least half an hour. **TIP:** Dab your cloth or chamois to remove any streaks that occurred when you wiped the glaze off. If you feel you missed any areas, let the first coat dry, and then go back and rework those areas. (If you try to re-coat before your urn or column is dry, you will damage the first coat.)

4 To add dimension and accentuate the high points of the relief, you will want to bring back some of the base color. To do this, dip a stencil brush in the base color paint and dab it on a paper towel to remove the excess paint. Brush over the high points of the relief and shade in some of the flat areas. Take your time and be patient with this step. Do not overload the brush. It is important that the top coat color be seen in the low points of the relief.

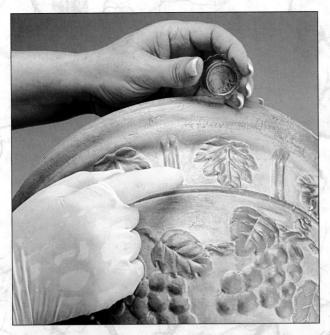 

5 Using the stencil brush, repeat Step 4, this time using the copper Liquid Leaf paint. Let dry, then follow by applying a bit of the colored wax with a gloved fingertip on the areas that you want to highlight further. TIP: The change in the shades between the copper and gold creates a very rich effect. Use them sparingly at first and then go back and add more.

6 Adding an antique glaze to your pillars will produce a more realistic patina or aged look. To do this, mix 1 tablespoon burnt umber tint with 2 cups clear glaze. Using the chip brush, apply the glaze mixture on the urn and the column, working in small sections as you did in Step 2. Pay close attention to the relief areas. Wipe off excess glaze from the high points of the relief using a soft cloth or chamois. If you feel you have too much glaze in the lower parts of the relief, use a small, dry brush to remove it. Dab your cloth or chamois to remove any streaks that were created from wiping the glaze off.

SPECIAL PROJECT TIP

• Patinas are used to create the look of a timeworn decorative piece. As you work on Steps 4, 5, and 6, stand back often and look at the piece. Where would colors be more worn or more prominent? Shadow and highlight areas in order to create a more realistic effect of an aged piece. For example, we added more base-coat color to the base of the urn because we felt in an outdoor setting, this area would naturally be less exposed to sunlight and wear.

Index

A

Altered Books, 74–75
American Style, 44–45
Art in the Garden, 42–43
Autumn Chill-Chaser, 94–97
Autumn Splendor, 32–35

B

Baskets
    A Spa Gift Basket, 98–99
Bead crafts
    Art in the Garden, 42–43
    A Garden Spindle, 40–41
Bedspreads
    Rise and Shine Bedspread, 16–17
Birdhouses
    Indoor Art, 76–77
Books
    Altered Books, 74–75
    Fun and Funky Photo Albums,
        88–91
    A Memorable Vacation, 70–73
Braided Past, 26–29

C

Candles and lights
    Center of Attention, 150–151
    Creative Candles, 114–116
    The Holidays by Candlelight,
        122–125
    The Luminous Pumpkin, 54–57
    Luxurious Lighting, 152–153
Card Art, 108–109
Casual Style
    Autumn Splendor, 32–35
    Braided Past, 26–29
    A Chair with a Flair, 22–23
    A Dressed-up Dresser, 8–9
    A Faux Stone Plaque, 30–31
    5 Minutes and Fabulous, 24–25
    Girly Fun, 14–15
    Instant Updates, 18–19
    A Personal Stamp, 10–11
    Rise and Shine Bedspread, 16–17
    Second Life, 12–13
    Vintage Memories, 20–21
Ceiling treatments
    A Crowning Touch, 146–147
Center of Attention, 150–151
Centerpiece

Center of Attention, 150–151
5 Minutes and Fabulous, 50–51
The Holidays by Candlelight,
    122–125
A Chair with a Flair, 22–23
Cheery Chairs, 140–143
Classic Decorating
    Center of Attention, 150–151
    Cheery Chairs, 140–143
    Comfortable Dining, 138–157
    A Crowning Touch, 146–147
    Delightful Details, 148–149
    Instant Age, 154–157
    Luxurious Lighting, 152–153
    Pro Faux, 132–135
    A Relaxed Meal, 144–145
    Simply elegant, 136–137
Comfortable Dining, 138–157
    Center of Attention, 150–151
    Cheery Chairs, 140–143
    A Crowning Touch, 146–147
    Delightful Details, 148–149
    Instant Age, 154–157
    Luxurious Lighting, 152–153
    A Relaxed Meal, 144–145
Containers. *See* Storage and display
Creative Candles, 114–116
Crochet
    Autumn Chill-Chaser, 94–97
    basic stitches, 95
A Crowning Touch, 146–147

D

Decorating
    Center of Attention, 150–151
    Cheery Chairs, 140–143
    Comfortable Dining, 138–157
    A Crowning Touch, 146–147
    Delightful Details, 148–149
    Dressed for the Season, 62–65
    Instant Age, 154–157
    Luxurious Lighting, 152–153
    Pro Faux, 132–135
    A Relaxed Meal, 144–145
    Simply elegant, 136–137
Decoupage
    Decoupage Flower Plate, 38–39
    Indoor Art, 76–77
Decoupage Flower Plate, 38–39
Delightful Details, 148–149
Dressed for the Season, 62–65

A Dressed-up Dresser, 8–9

E

Embroidery
    Autumn Splendor, 32–35
    basic stitches for, 81–82
    A Thistle Purse, 80–83

F

Fabric crafts
    Autumn Splendor, 32–35
    Braided Past, 26–29
    Cheery Chairs, 140–143
    5 Minutes and Fabulous, 24–25
    A Frosty Pillow, 100–101
    Gifts for Giving, 106–107
    A Memory Pillow, 78–79
    A Painted Garden Tote, 66–67
    A Picnic Bench Cushion, 52–53
    Rise and Shine Bedspread, 16–17
    Second Life, 12–13
    Simply elegant, 136–137
    A Spa Gift Basket, 98–99
    A Thistle Purse, 80–83
    A Victorian Christmas, 126–129
    Vintage Christmas Ornaments,
        118–121
    Vintage Memories, 20–21
Faux finishes, 132–135
A Faux Stone Plaque, 30–31
5 Minutes and Fabulous, 24–25,
    50–51
Floor coverings
    Braided Past, 26–29
Floral arrangements
    5 Minutes and Fabulous, 50–51
Flowers, dried
    Decoupage Flower Plate, 38–39
A Frosty Pillow, 100–101
Fun and Funky Photo Albums, 88–91
Furniture
    A Chair with a Flair, 22–23
    Cheery Chairs, 140–143
    Instant Updates, 18–19

G

A Garden Spindle, 40–41
Gifts. *See* Mementos & Gifts
Gifts for Giving, 106–107

Girly Fun, 14–15
Glass crafts
    Decoupage Flower Plate, 38–39
    The Holidays by Candlelight,
        122–125
    Luxurious Lighting, 152–153
    A Personal Stamp, 10–11
    Personal Style, 116–117
Gloves
    A Spa Gift Basket, 98–99

H

Handmade Holiday Greetings,
    112–113
Hat
    Autumn Chill-Chaser, 94–97
Holiday cards
    Handmade Holiday Greetings,
        112–113
Holiday Events
    Creative Candles, 114–116
    Handmade Holiday Greetings,
        112–113
    The Holidays by Candlelight,
        122–125
    Personal Style, 116–117
    A Victorian Christmas, 126–129
    Vintage Christmas Ornaments,
        118–121
The Holidays by Candlelight,
    122–125

I

Indoor Art, 76–77
Instant Age, 154–157
Instant Updates, 18–19
Invitations
    Wedding Season, 84–87

J

Jewelry
    Your Own Domino Jewelry,
        102–105

L

Lighting. *See also* Candles and lights
    Luxurious Lighting, 152–153
The Luminous Pumpkin, 54–57
Luxurious Lighting, 152–153

M

Mementos & Gifts

Altered Books, 74–75
Autumn Chill-Chaser, 94–97
Card Art, 108–109
A Frosty Pillow, 100–101
Fun and Funky Photo Albums,
    88–91
Gifts for Giving, 106–107
Indoor Art, 76–77
A Memorable Vacation, 70–73
A Memory Pillow, 78–79
A Personal Shadow Box, 92–93
A Spa Gift Basket, 98–99
A Thistle Purse, 80–83
Wedding Season, 84–87
Your Own Domino Jewelry,
    102–105
A Memorable Vacation, 70–73
A Memory Pillow, 78–79
Mobile
    Art in the Garden, 42–43

N

Napkin rings
    5 Minutes and Fabulous, 24–25
Natural Beauty
    American Style, 44–45
    Art in the Garden, 42–43
    Decoupage Flower Plate, 38–39
    Dressed for the Season, 62–65
    5 Minutes and Fabulous, 50–51
    A Garden Spindle, 40–41
    The Luminous Pumpkin, 54–57
    A Painted Garden Tote, 66–67
    Perfect Pots, 46–47
    A Picnic Bench Cushion, 52–53
    Rings of Nature, 58–61
    A Window Box Table, 48–49
Necklaces
    Your Own Domino Jewelry,
        102–105

O

Ornaments
    Personal Style, 116–117
    Vintage Christmas Ornaments,
        118–121

P

A Painted Garden Tote, 66–67
Painting crafts
    American Style, 44–45
    A Chair with a Flair, 22–23
    Cheery Chairs, 140–143
    A Dressed-up Dresser, 8–9

Girly Fun, 14–15
Indoor Art, 76–77
Instant Age, 154–157
A Painted Garden Tote, 66–67
Perfect Pots, 46–47
Pro Faux, 132–135
Rise and Shine Bedspread, 16–17
Wedding Season, 84–87
Your Own Domino Jewelry,
    102–105
Paper crafts
    Altered Books, 74–75
    Card Art, 108–109
    Creative Candles, 114–116
    A Dressed-up Dresser, 8–9
    Fun and Funky Photo Albums,
        88–91
    Handmade Holiday Greetings,
        112–113
    A Memorable Vacation, 70–73
    Wedding Season, 84–87
    Perfect Pots, 46–47
A Personal Shadow Box, 92–93
A Personal Stamp, 10–11
Personal Style, 116–117
Photo storage/display
    Fun and Funky Photo Albums,
        88–91
    A Personal Shadow Box, 92–93
A Picnic Bench Cushion, 52–53
Pillars
    Instant Age, 154–157
Pillows
    Autumn Splendor, 32–35
    A Frosty Pillow, 100–101
    Gifts for Giving, 106–107
    A Memory Pillow, 78–79
    A Picnic Bench Cushion, 52–53
    A Relaxed Meal, 144–145
    Second Life, 12–13
Pins
    Your Own Domino Jewelry,
        102–105
Plaque
    A Faux Stone Plaque, 30–31
Plates
    Decoupage Flower Plate, 38–39
    A Personal Stamp, 10–11
Pots
    Perfect Pots, 46–47
Pro Faux, 132–135
Pumpkins
    The Luminous Pumpkin, 54–57
Purse
    A Thistle Purse, 80–83

R

A Relaxed Meal, 144–145
Rings of Nature, 58–61
Rise and Shine Bedspread, 16–17
Rub-on transfers
Instant Updates, 18–19
Rugs
Braided Past, 26–29

S

Scarf
Autumn Chill-Chaser, 94–97
Sculpting
Delightful Details, 148–149
A Faux Stone Plaque, 30–31
Second Life, 12–13
Sewing crafts
Autumn Splendor, 32–35
A Frosty Pillow, 100–101
Gifts for Giving, 106–107
A Memory Pillow, 78–79
A Picnic Bench Cushion, 52–53
Rise and Shine Bedspread, 16–17
Second Life, 12–13
A Spa Gift Basket, 98–99
A Thistle Purse, 80–83
A Victorian Christmas, 126–129
Vintage Christmas Ornaments,
116–121
Vintage Memories, 20–21
Shelves
Instant Updates, 18–19
Simply elegant, 136–137
A Spa Gift Basket, 98–99

Stamping, 66–67
Creative Candles, 114–116
Gifts for Giving, 106–107
Girly Fun, 14–15
Handmade Holiday Greetings,
112–113
A Personal Stamp, 10–11
Rise and Shine Bedspread, 16–17
Stenciling
A Chair with a Flair, 22–23
Delightful Details, 148–149
A Frosty Pillow, 100–101
Perfect Pots, 46–47
Storage and display
Altered Books, 74–75
American Style, 44–45
5 Minutes and Fabulous, 50–51
Fun and Funky Photo Albums,
88–91
A Memorable Vacation, 70–73
Perfect Pots, 46–47
A Personal Shadow Box, 92–93
Rings of Nature, 58–61
A Window Box Table, 48–49

T

A Thistle Purse, 80–83

V

Vases
5 Minutes and Fabulous, 50–51
The Luminous Pumpkin, 54–57
A Victorian Christmas, 126–129

Vintage Christmas Ornaments,
118–121
Vintage Memories, 20–21

W

Wall finishes
Pro Faux, 132–135
Wastebasket
Girly Fun, 14–15
Wedding Season, 84–87
Window box
Dressed for the Season, 62–65
A Window Box Table, 48–49
A Window Box Table, 48–49
Window treatments
Simply elegant, 136–137
Vintage Memories, 20–21
Wine caddy
Rings of Nature, 58–61
Wire craft
A Garden Spindle, 40–41
Wood crafts
American Style, 44–45
Center of Attention, 150–151
A Dressed-up Dresser, 8–9
A Garden Spindle, 40–41
Rings of Nature, 58–61
A Window Box Table, 48–49

Y

Your Own Domino Jewelry, 102–105